"I MADE IT MYSELF!"

"I MADE IT MYSELF!"

Harriet W. Hodgson

Illustrations by Teena Remer

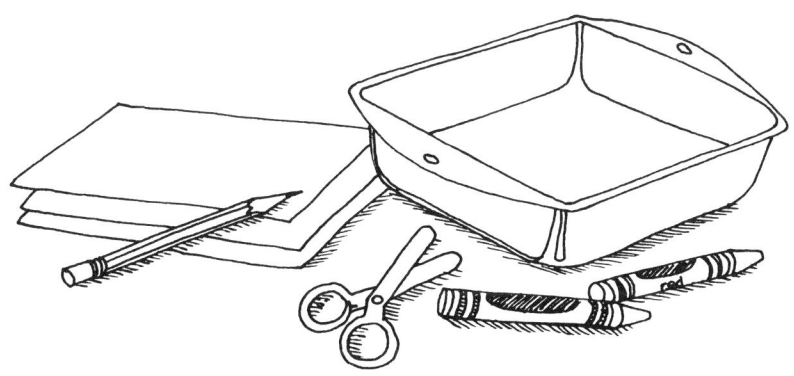

WARNER/B. LANSKY BOOKS
A Warner Communications Company

WARNER BOOKS EDITION

Copyright © 1979 by Harriet W. Hodgson
All rights reserved

Published by arrangement with B. Lansky Books

A Warner Communications Company

Warner Books, Inc.
75 Rockefeller Plaza
New York, N.Y. 10019

Illustrations: Teena Remer
Cover Photography: Thoen Photography
Photography: Glenn Hagen
Cover and Book Design: Cathleen Casey

Library of Congress Cataloging in Publication Data

Hodgson, Harriet W.
　"I Made It Myself!"
　Includes index.
　SUMMARY: Instructions for making dozens of toys from "junk that most of us have."
　1. Toy making — Juvenile literature. 2. Handicraft — Juvenile literature. [1. Toy making. 2. Handicraft] I. Title.
　TT174.H63   745.59'2   79-12916
　ISBN 0-446-97083-2

Printed in the United States of America

First Printing: October, 1979

10 9 8 7 6 5 4 3 2

CONTENTS

Letter to Children	1
Letter to Parents	2
Alpha-Circles	3
Animal Crackers	4
Apple Basket	5
Art Tote	6
Big Boat, Little Boat	7
Bottle Bowling	8
Button and Cup Toy	9
Cake Bake	10
Canned Consonants	11
Car Kit	13
Catch Ball	14
Cereal Box Puzzles	15
Clippety-Snippety	16
Clothespin Drop	17
Clothespin Words	18
Cockeyed Comics	19
Crazy Car	21
Cylinder Ball	22
Cylinder Soldiers	23
Dandy Dishes	24
Detective	25
Dolly's Dolly	27
Don't Tickle a Trout	28
Eggs Plus	29
Faces and Feelings	30
Four Score	31
Free Flyer	32
Funny Fences	33
Giant Grocery Cart	35
Gone Fishin'	36
Hat Box	37
How Long?	38
Jumpscotch	39
Learn-to-Button Animals	41
Lid Toss	42
Little Bubbles	43
Lunchbox	44
Macaroni Match	45
Magazine Picture Dictionary	46
Marble Track	47
Moon People	49
Musical Door Hook	50
My Book	51
Name Worm	52
Nothing-to-Do Cards	53
Plain Plane	55
Play Stove	56
Playday Playclay	57
Playhouse	59
Rainbow Book	60
Rhymers	61
Ring-O	62
Sand Pendulum	63
Shadow Puppets	65
Shape Sorting	66
Silly Eggs	67
Space Helmet	69
Spongy Blocks	70
Stars-in-the-Moon Mobile	71
Stickeroo	72
Stitcheroo	73
Stop Light	75
Story Spinner	76
Super Scoop	77
Target Toss	78
Terrific Target	79
Tic-Tac-Tops	81
Toothpaste	82
Vegetable Soup	83
Wash-Me Mit	84
Washing Machine	85
Whirl-O	86
Wooden Spoon Doll	87
Writing Kit	89
Supply Chest	90

Dedicated to the children
of Aldrich Memorial Nursery School
Rochester, Minnesota

Hey Kids,

Wanna know a secret? The secret is about this book. The secret is that it's yours. Yeah. YOURS! There are lots of pictures. There are few words.

This is a DOING book. Not a sitting-sighing, moaning-groaning book. Not this one. Instead, this is a really fun and get it done book.

Are you sick of watching T. V.? Are you bored because your best buddy is gone? Are you mad because the dog doesn't play checkers? Are you stuck inside because rotten weather is stuck outside? Then this book is for you.

All of the toys are made from stuff-around-the-house. Stuff that most of us have. If you don't have the stuff shown in the pictures, use what you DO have. That will make you a toy inventor. Wow!

There's no need to worry about these toys. No need to feel bad if someone sits or steps on them. The toys can easily be made again and half the fun is in the making. Just look around for more jazzy junk.

Play by yourself or with the gang on the block. Be a friend and share the toys. Be a friend and share the book. It's YOURS!

That's the secret.

Dear Parents,

This book is for kids and you, too. I wrote it because "I've been there." I've had lots of dandy days.

Days when the washing machine overflowed, the dog had the flu, the baby stuck a Japanese doll up her nose, the car smokily self-destructed, the groceries were gone and the sun wasn't up yet!

Obviously, help was needed. Help that was both practical and quick. But where do you find it?

Some books try to help. Craft books for kids that are supposed to solve the Saturday bluckies and the Sunday mess. With most of them you need to be a graduate engineer or a direct descendant of Leonardo da Vinci. Better yet, both!

This book is different. If offers:

> CREATIVE projects for kids
> QUICK projects for kids
> QUALITY projects for kids
> CHEAP projects for kids

Best of all, the toys are made from stuff that's lying around the house. Stuff that you've already paid for: egg cartons, margarine tubs, tin cans, plastic bottles, boxes and bits of string. There's a list in the back of the book of other things you can start saving. If you've paid for 'em you might as well use 'em!

Super-simple toy directions yield quick results. The toys take only minutes to make and one toy takes no time at all. Occasionally the directions call for adult help. Don't panic.

Such help is minimal. You can share cozy, quality time with your kids and then return to perusing the paper or having dinner. After the toys are made there will still be a you left. That's important.

Toy designs are open-ended. There are no absolutes. Please add a generous dash of individual imagination. If the completed projects don't look like the pictures, hooray! Then the toys truly reflect the toymakers.

You say the hamster is missing, the kids bubble gummed each other, the dog walked in with a crew cut, supper's burned black, the house is a disaster area and the forecast is thunder bumpers followed by rain? Then it's time to pick a project and start having fun.

Harriet W. Hodgson

Alpha-Circles

What you need:

26 tops from gallon-size plastic milk bottles
3 egg cartons
marking pen
rubber band

What you do:

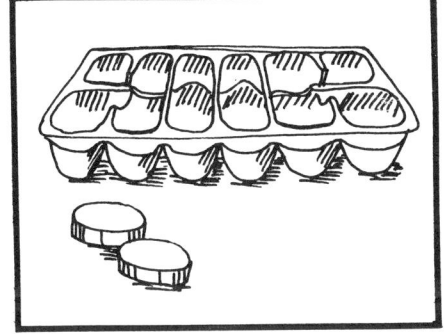

1 Rinse and dry the milk bottle tops.

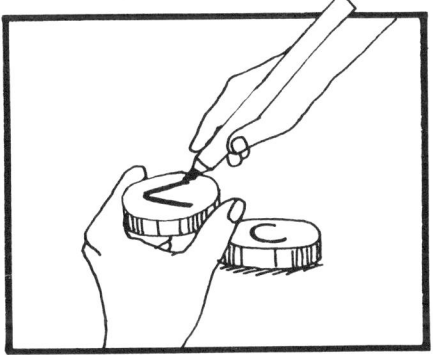

2 Print one alphabet letter on each bottle top with marking pen. These are the alpha-circles.

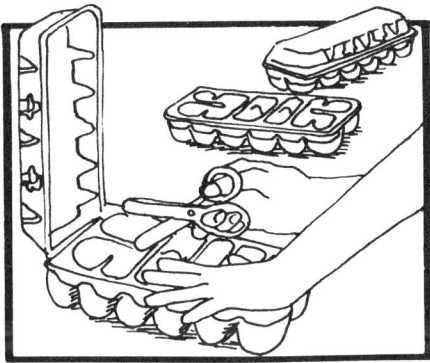

3 Cut the lids off of 2 egg cartons, leaving the third one whole.

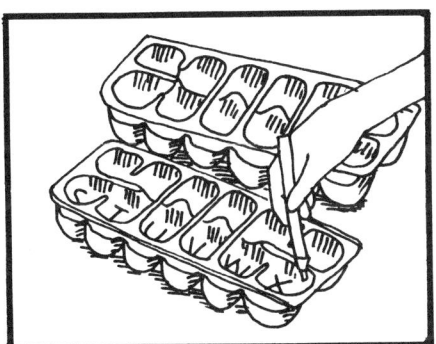

4 Print one alphabet letter in the bottom of each bump of the egg carton. The third egg carton will only have y and z.

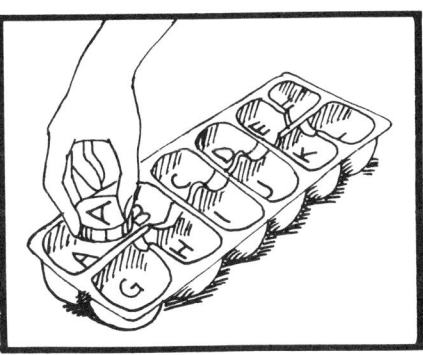

5 Match the letters, putting the alpha-circle on top of its match in the egg carton.

6 Store the alpha-circles in the lidded egg carton. Hold the other cartons beneath it with a rubber band.

Animal Crackers

What you need:

- box of animal crackers
- pencil
- scissors
- glue
- spring-type clothespins (wooden)
- margarine tubs

What you do:

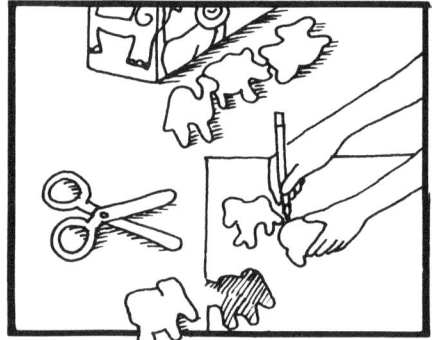

1 Take 1 of each shape cracker out of the box. Trace around the crackers with pencil.

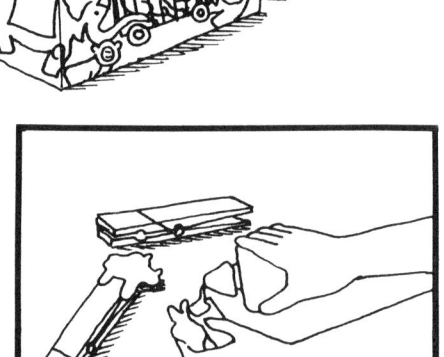

2 Cut out the paper crackers. Paste each cracker on a clothespin.

3 Snap each clothespin onto a margarine tub to show where the crackers go.

4 Sort the rest of the crackers into the right margarine tubs.

Of course you should munch a few.

Apple Basket

What you need:

peel-strip juice can lids
crayons
pencil
cardboard
1 die
margarine tub with lid

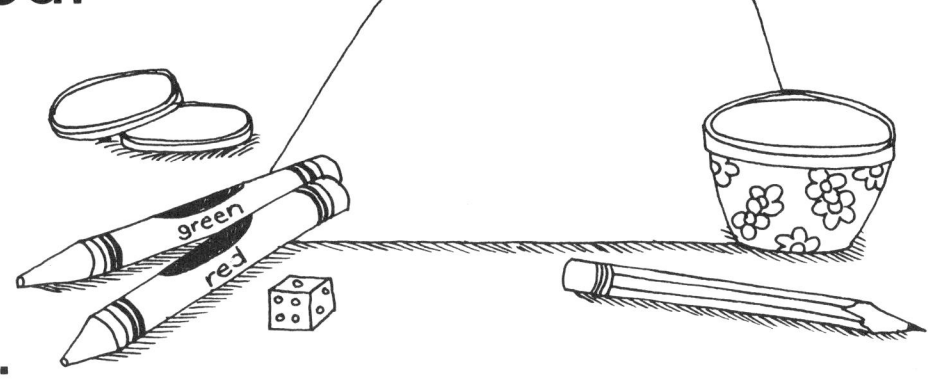

What you do:

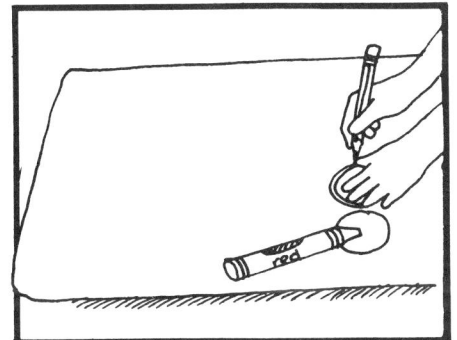

1 Rinse and dry juice can lids. Use one lid to help you draw a row of circles that curves from one edge of the cardboard to the other.

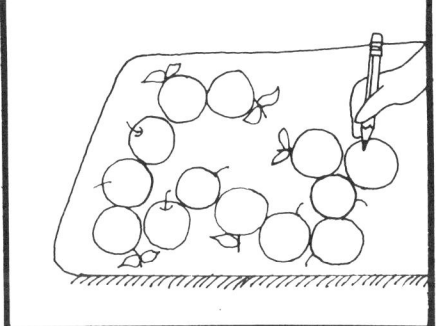

2 To make the circles look like apples, draw stems on them and color them.

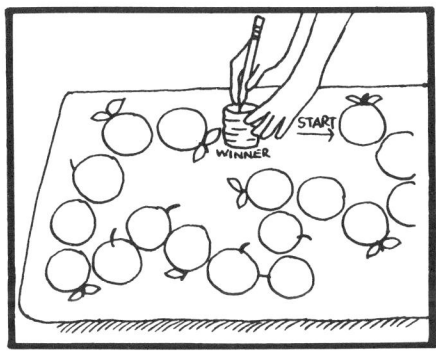

3 Draw an arrow in the first circle to mark the start of the game and a basket in the last circle to mark the end of the game.

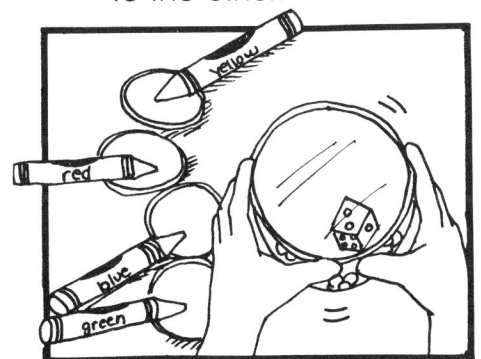

4 Use juice can lids as your markers. Code each with a different color crayon. Put a die in the margarine tub and snap on the lid.

5 Take turns shaking the die. If 1 dot shows on the top of the die, move the marker 1 circle toward the basket. If 2 dots show, move 2 circles, and so on.

Want an apple?

Art Tote

What you need:

plastic cleaning caddy
 (with a center handle)
or cardboard soft-drink carton
all sorts of art stuff

What you do:

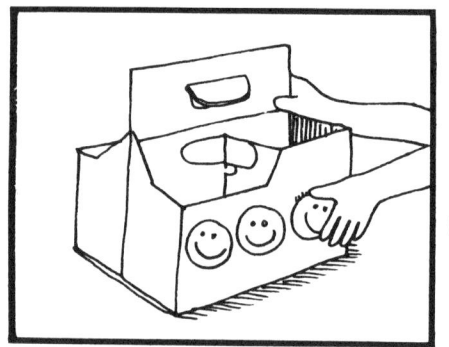

1 Buy a plastic cleaning caddy. They don't cost much and you can find them in lots of stores. Or use a soft-drink carton. Decorate your tote to make it more interesting.

2 Fill the tote with art stuff: crayons, Magic Markers, pencil, paste, scissors, drawing paper, colored paper, stickers, tissue paper, bits of cloth.

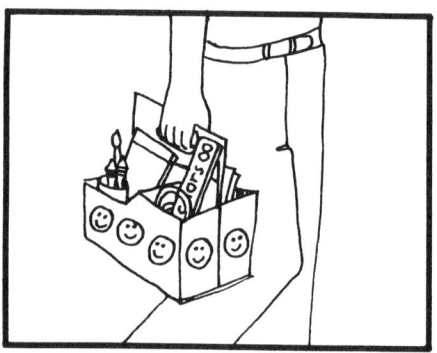

3 Use the art tote any time you feel like making something.

You can make more totes to carry other things.

Big Boat, Little Boat

What you need:

wooden scrub brush
wooden nail brush
big spool
little spool
glue
shoelace

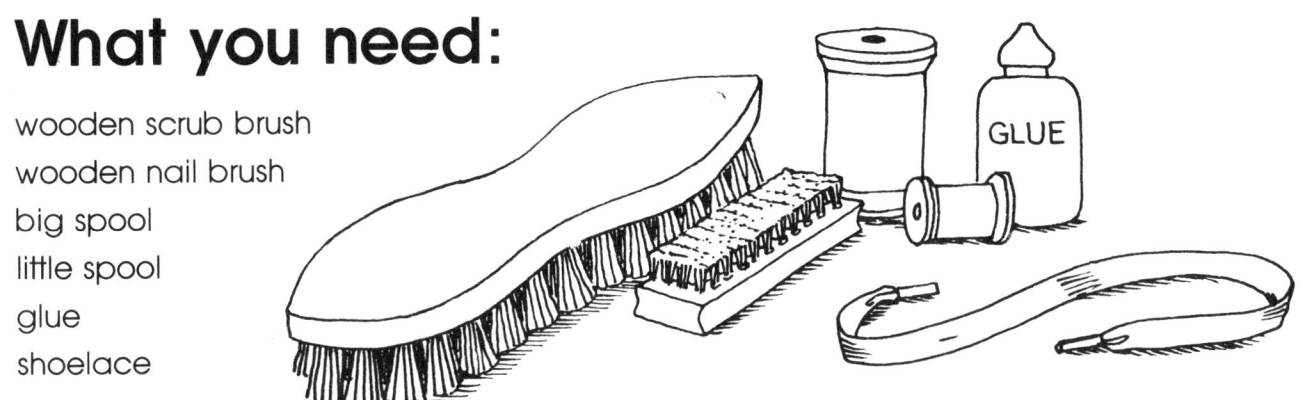

What you do:

1 Glue the big spool onto the big brush. Glue the little spool onto the little brush.

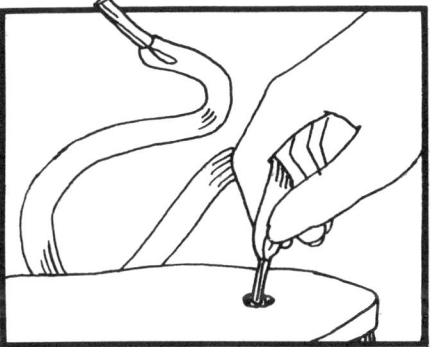

2 Poke a shoelace through the hole in the big brush so you can pull your boat through the water.

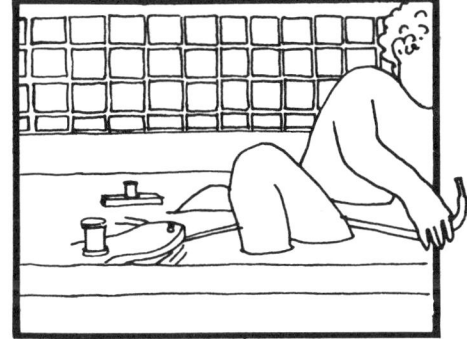

3 Make waves in the water with your boats.

How about scrubbing the ring off the bathtub before you hop out?

Bottle Bowling

What you need:

ball
empty detergent bottles (same size)

What you do:

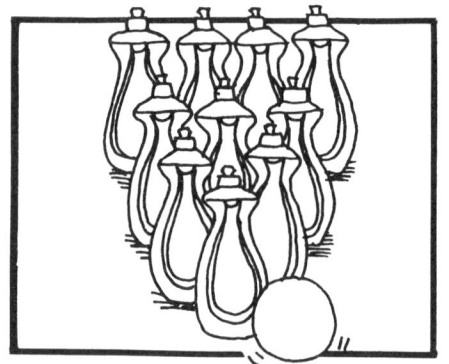

1 Rinse and dry the bottles. Set them on the floor like bowling pins.

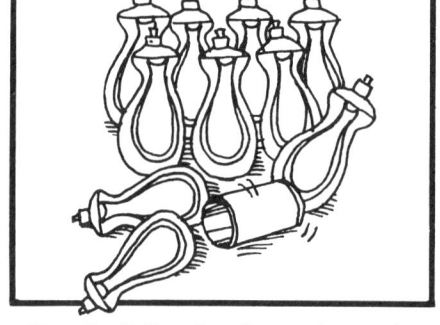

2 Roll the ball and see how many bottles you can knock down. No ball? Roll an empty can.

How many can you knock down at once?

Button and Cup Toy

What you need:

Styrofoam cup
nail
button
string

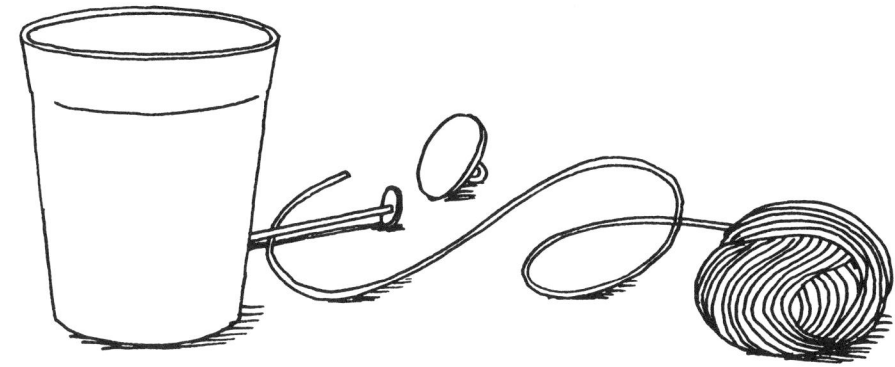

What you do:

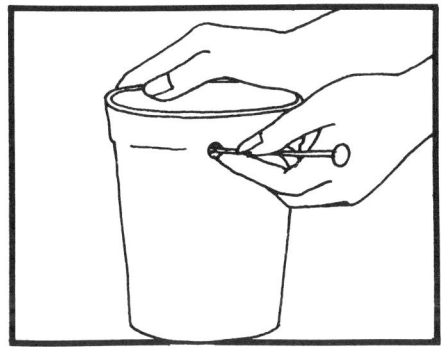

1 Use a nail to punch a hole close to the rim of the Styrofoam cup.

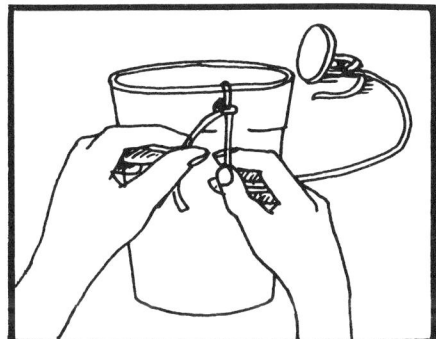

2 Tie one end of the string to the cup and the other end to a large button.

3 Swing the string slowly and catch the button in the cup. Don't make the string too long or you'll catch your nose!

See how many times you can catch the button without missing!

Cake Bake

What you need:

colored paper
pencil
scissors
square cake pan

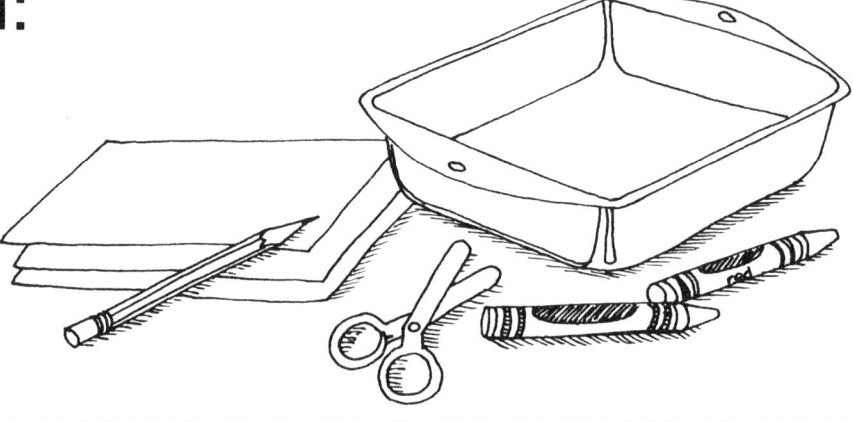

What you do:

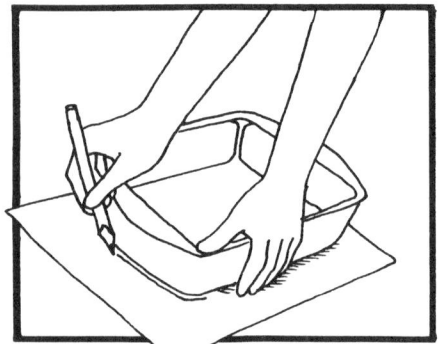

1 Trace around the bottom of the cake pan on colored paper.

2 Cut to fit the pan.

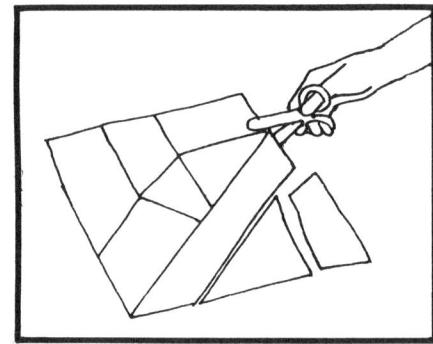

3 Cut each square into puzzle pieces.

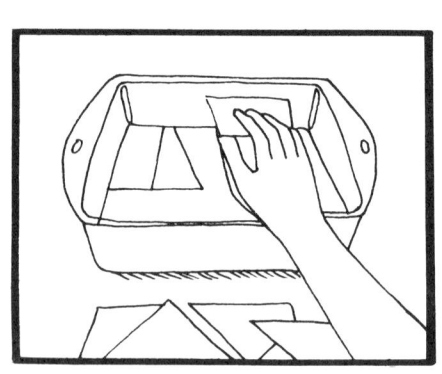

4 Do your square puzzles in the pan.

What did you bake today? You've been busy!

Canned Consonants

What you need:

coffee can
lots of plastic lids
ball-point pen
household stuff

What you do:

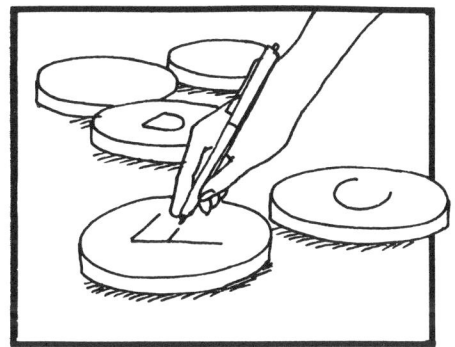

1 Use the pen to print a consonant letter on each coffee can lid.

2 Search around the house for small things that begin with that letter.

3 Put them all in the can and snap on the lid. Shake them up, dump 'em out and do it again with another lid.

You've got canned consonants! Care to try canned vowels?

Car Kit

What you need:

cardboard box with lid
newspaper comics
felt
glue
pencil
paper
trash bag ties

What you do:

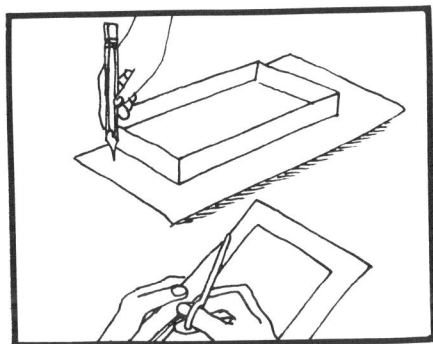

1 Trace the box lid on felt and cut out the rectangle.

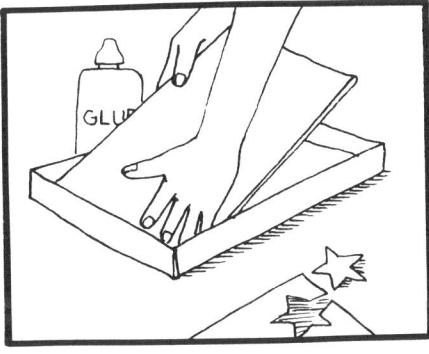

2 Glue the rectangle to the inside of the lid. Cut out all kinds of shapes from felt.

3 Look around for anything that sticks to felt: cotton balls, yarn, ric-rac, etc. Use all of these things to make pictures by pressing them to the felt background.

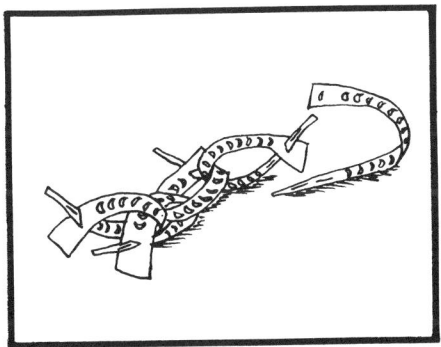

4 Link the trash bag ties into a chain.

5 Draw with the pencil on the paper. Look at the comics and munch on your snack.

Have a good trip!

Catch-Ball

What you need:

plastic milk bottles
kitchen shears
ball

What you do:

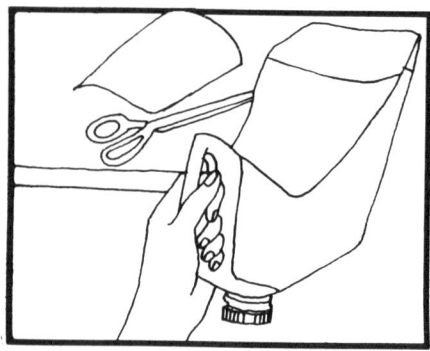

1 Cut the bottom off each plastic milk bottle, slanting up toward the handle. Leave the handle on. These are the catching scoops.

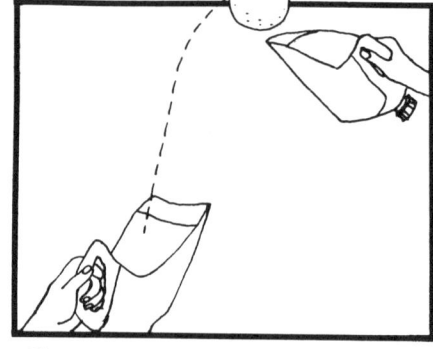

2 Use the scoops to play catch with a ball. No ball? Throw a sponge.

More than two people can play. When you get really good you can play hot-potato!

Cereal Box Puzzles

What you need:

empty cereal boxes
scissors
crayons
envelopes

What you do:

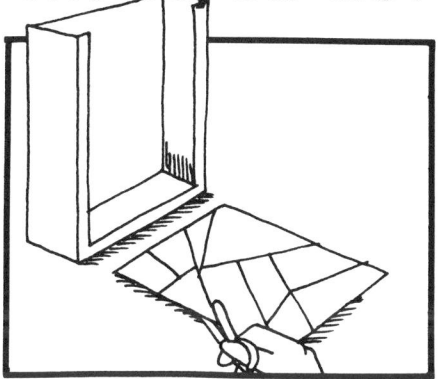

1 Carefully cut the front off each cereal box.

2 Cut the box front into puzzle shapes.

3 With crayons, color code pieces on the back so they won't get mixed up. Keep each puzzle in its own envelope.

Mini puzzles can be made from tiny pudding and cereal boxes.

Clippety-Snippety

What you need:

large brown envelope
pen
colored paper
scrap paper
scissors
paste

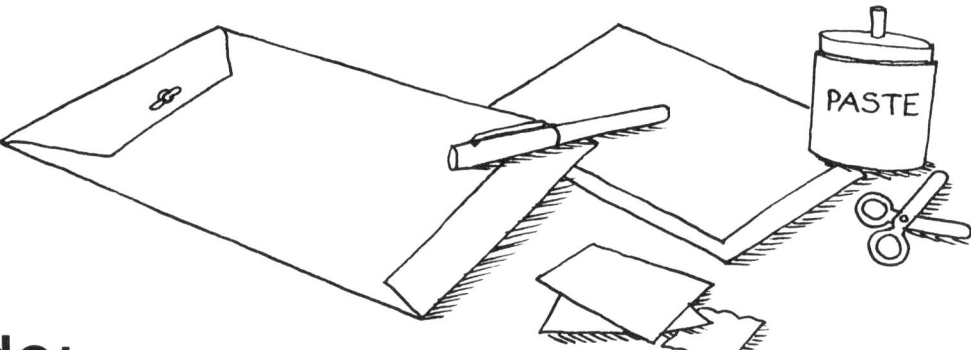

What you do:

1 Print the names of the different kinds of cuts you can make with scissors on the outside of an envelope — fringing, straight, folded, etc.

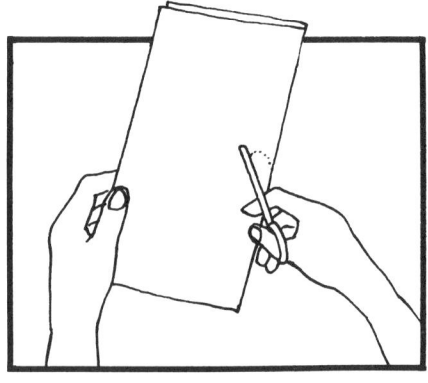

2 Make a sample of each kind of cutting with colored paper, like a Valentine for folded cutting.

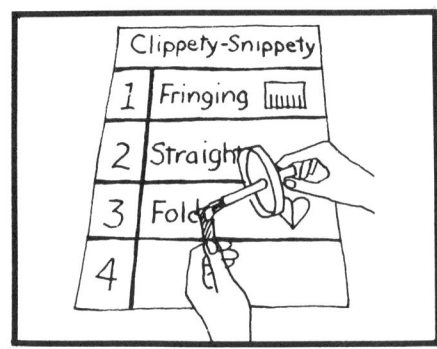

3 Paste each sample of cutting by its name to help you remember it.

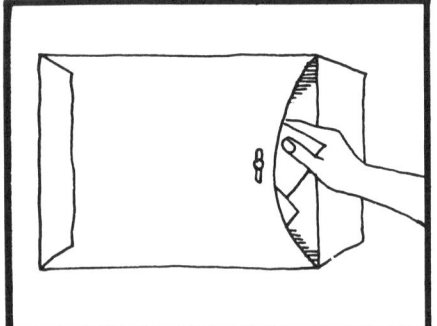

4 Put scissors and scrap paper in the envelope. Use clippety-snippety whenever you feel like cutting.

Paper cutting is great for rainy days.

Clothespin Drop

What you need:

plastic milk bottle
kitchen shears
clothespins

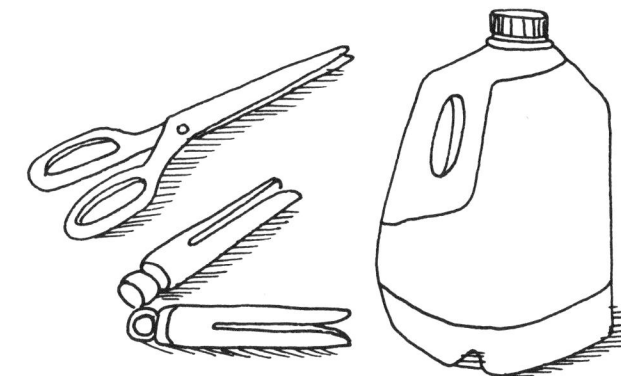

What you do:

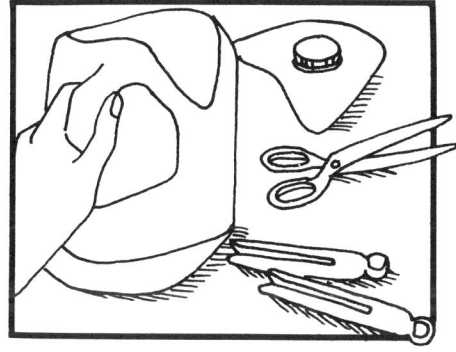

1 Cut a hole in the top of the plastic milk bottle. Remember to leave the handle on.

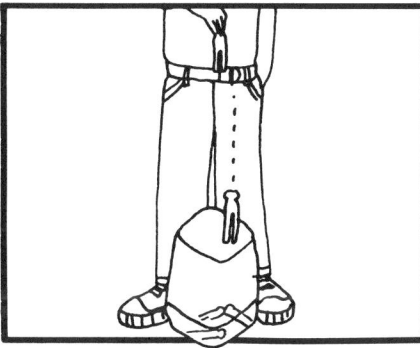

2 Find some old clothespins. Keeping your legs straight, stand over the milk bottle and see how many clothespins you can drop through the hole. Hurray!

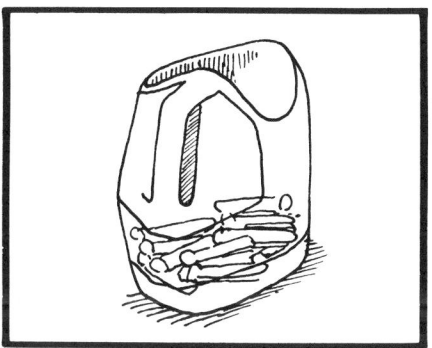

3 Keep the clothespins inside the milk bottle until you play another day.

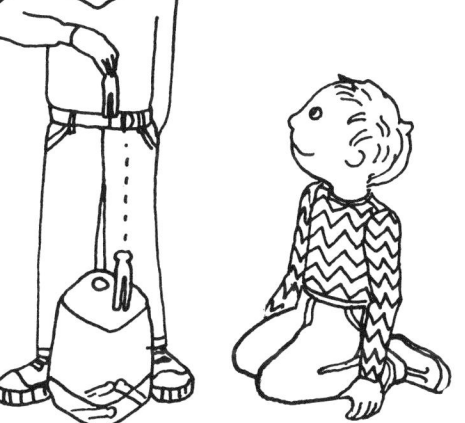

No milk bottle? What else could you use?

Clothespin Words

What you need:

hanger
permanent marker
spring-type clothespins
    (wooden)

What you do:

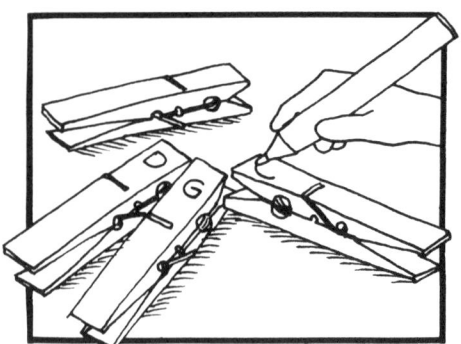

1 Print an alphabet letter on each clothespin. Include both vowels and consonants.

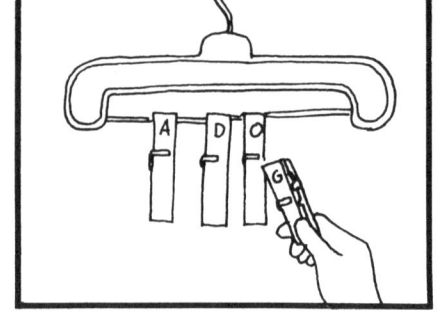

2 Make as many words as you can by snapping clothespins onto the hanger.

Play with a friend. Twice the fun! Time each other to see how many words you can each make in a minute.

Cockeyed Comics

What you need:

newspaper comics
scissors
paper
paste

What you do:

1 Find the comic pages. Cut one comic strip apart.

2 Paste the comic squares on paper, one per page. Scramble them.

3 Play three ways: picture "read" the comics and put them back together. If you can, read the words and put them back together. Or mix them up for cockeyed comics! Got a cockeyed story to go with 'em?

Tell your cockeyed stories to a friend. See if your friend can invent others!

19

Crazy Car

What you need:

plastic detergent bottle (without handle)
nail
4 plastic bottle tops (the same size)
2 pipe cleaners

What you do:

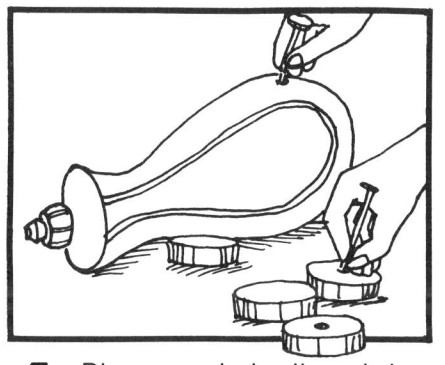

1 Rinse and dry the detergent bottle. Screw top back on. Use nail to punch 4 holes in bottle where you want the wheels to be. Make holes opposite each other.

2 Use nail to punch center holes in bottle tops. Push each pipe cleaner through the bottle to its matching hole on the other side.

3 A bottle top wheel goes on each end of each pipe cleaner. Twist pipe cleaner ends so wheels won't fall off.

Decide which is front and which is back, which is top and which is bottom. What a crazy car!

Cylinder Ball

What you need:

plastic ice cream bucket
kitchen shears
nails (the kind with flat tops)
sponge ball

What you do:

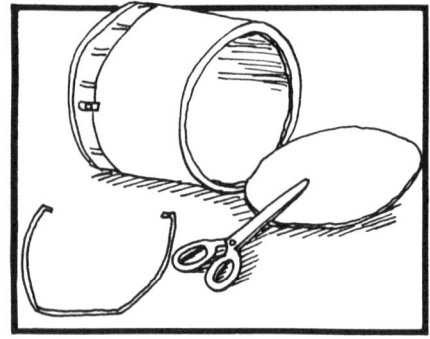

1 Use the kitchen shears to carefully cut the bottom off the ice cream bucket. The shape is now a cylinder. Slowly snap off the wire handle.

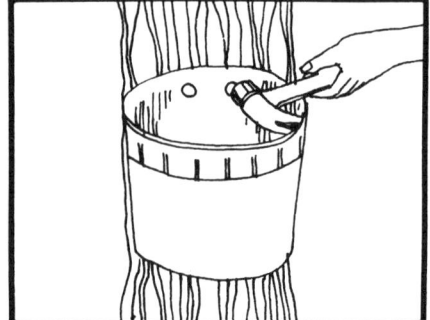

2 Nail the cylinder to a tree or post. Use it like a basketball net with a ball, sponge, or knotted sock.

You can draw or tape a net on, too.

Cylinder Soldiers

What you need:

cardboard tubes from toilet paper
colored paper
scissors
paste
permanent marker

What you do:

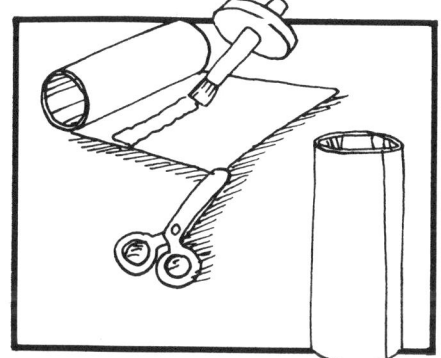

1 Cut colored paper to fit around the cardboard tubes.

2 Glue paper onto each tube.

3 Add a face with permanent marker. You've just made a soldier. Make an army of 'em!

March your soldiers in a parade and line them up for inspection. Attennnn-shun!

Dandy Dishes

What you need:

cardboard frozen juice cans (the peel-strip kind)
colored paper
glue
plastic lids
picnic silverware
paper napkins
old magazines
scissors
paste
cardboard

What you do:

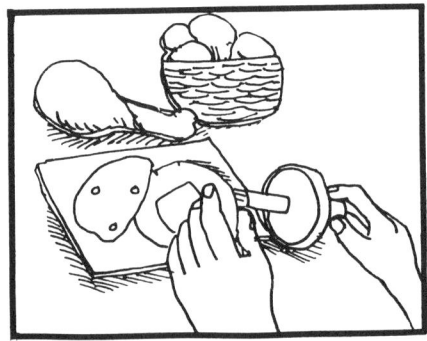
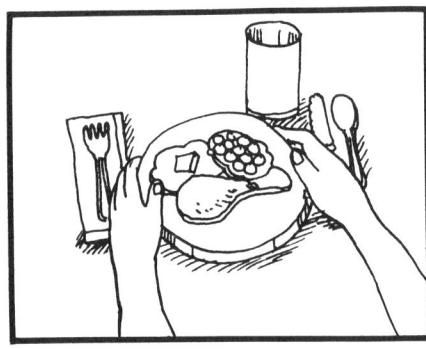

1 Rinse and dry the juice cans. Cut colored paper to fit the sides and glue on for party glasses. Use plastic lids as plates.

2 Cut out magazine pictures of food and paste onto cardboard. There's your pretend food!

3 Set the table with your dandy dishes, glasses, silverware, napkins and food because we're ready to eat. What's for supper?

Dolls and friends like tea parties and dinners served on your dandy dishes.

Detective

What you need:

plastic lid
scissors
spring-type clothespin

What you do:

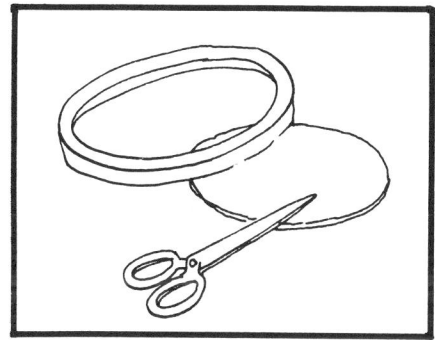

1 Cut out the center from the plastic lid, leaving the rim. This shape is a ring.

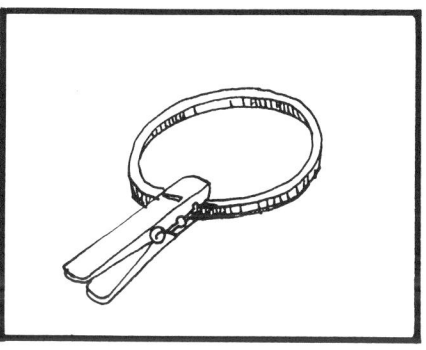

2 Snap a clothespin onto the ring to make a handle.

3 It looks like a magnifying glass, doesn't it? Be a detective. Search around your house. What do you see in the ring?

You can search for things that are the same color, things that are rough or smooth, and things that rhyme. You're some detective!

Dolly's Dolly

What you need:

old work glove
scissors
needle
thread
cotton balls
marker or ball-point pen

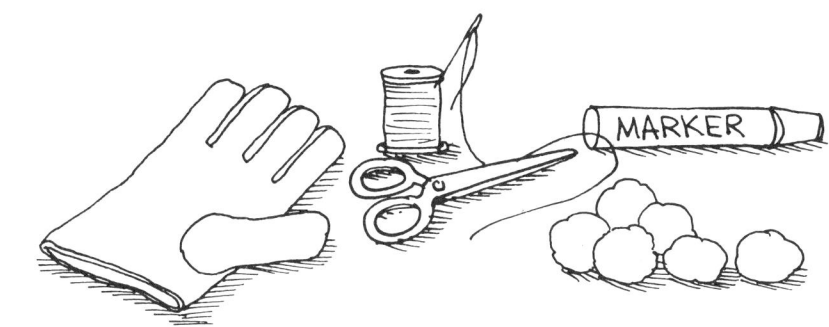

What you do:

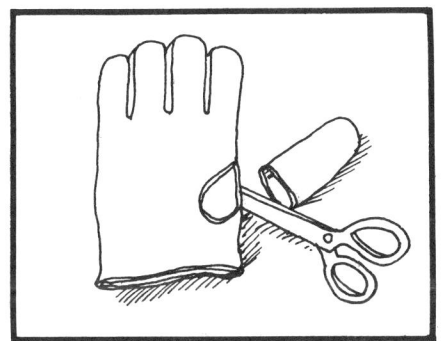

1 Cut the largest finger off an old work glove.

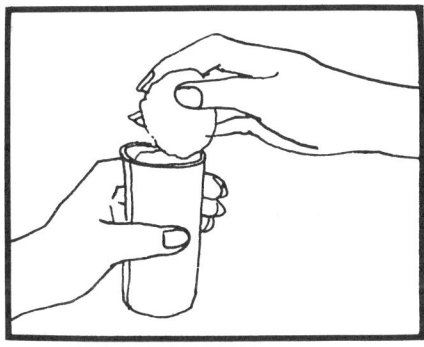

2 Stuff it with cotton balls.

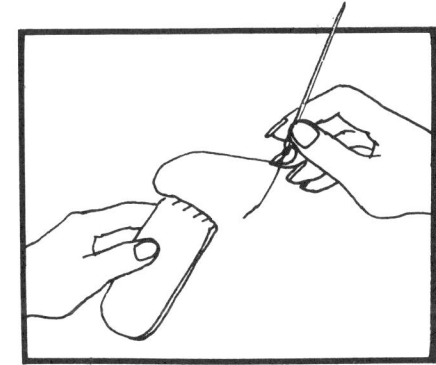

3 Stitch the open end closed.

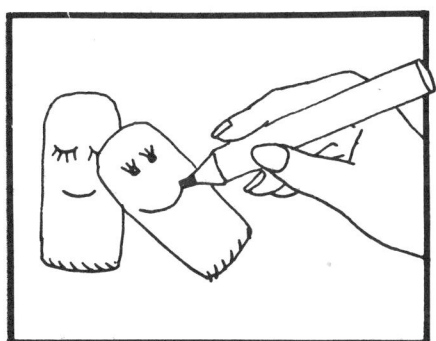

4 Use the permanent marker to draw two open eyes on one side of dolly, two closed eyes on the other.

Good night, sleep tight.

Don't Tickle a Trout!

What you need:

crayons
cardboard
two shoelaces

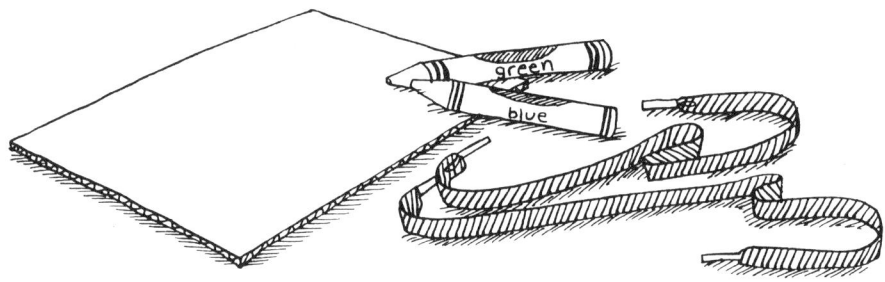

What you do:

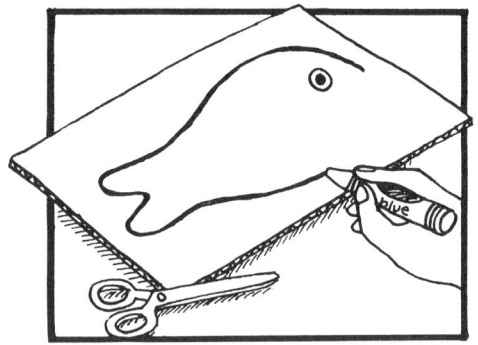

1 Draw a big fish shape on cardboard.

2 Put the fish on the floor with a shoelace on each side.

3 Jump across the shoelace "brook" without falling in. Each time someone jumps, the shoelaces are moved farther apart. Don't fall in and tickle a trout!

The last one to make a good jump is the winner.

Eggs Plus

What you need:

L'eggs stockings egg
permanent marker
paper

What you do:

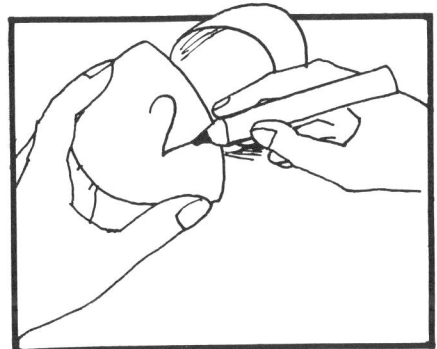

1 Open the egg. Print a number on the outside of the smaller half.

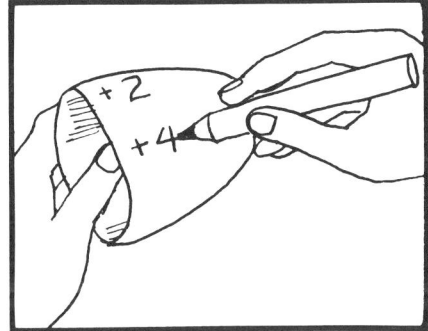

2 Print numbers on the outside of the larger half, such as +2, +4, and +6, to make number problems.

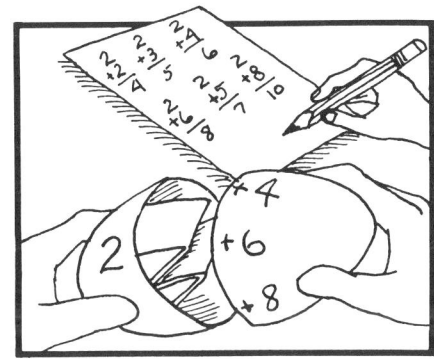

3 Print answers to the number problems, like 2 + 2 = 4, 2 + 6 = 8, on the paper. Hide the paper inside the egg.

4 Slowly turn the egg and line up the numbers. Now add the top number to the bottom ones. Can you guess the answers?

You could also subtract or multiply.

Faces and Feelings

What you need:

small paper plates
permanent marker
scissors
popsicle sticks
glue

What you do:

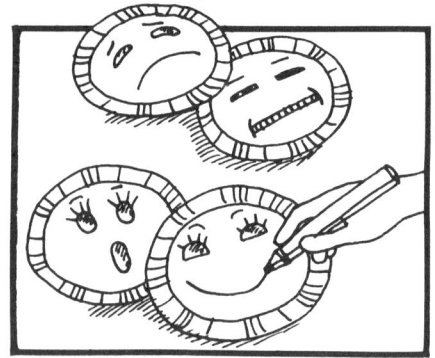

1 Draw a face on each paper plate. Make them all different: smiling mouth, sad mouth, open eyes, surprised eyes, etc.

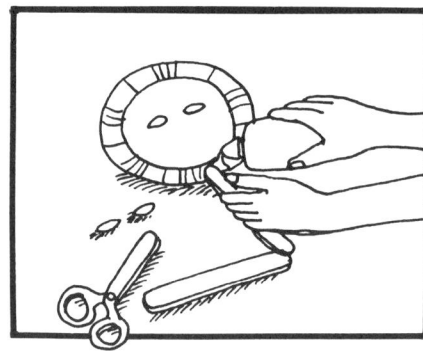

2 Cut out the eye spaces on each plate so you can see. Glue a popsicle stick onto each mask you've made.

3 Hold each mask up to your face and tell a story to go with it.

Did you scare yourself?

Four Score

What you need:

paper
pencil
1 die
margarine tub with lid

What you do:

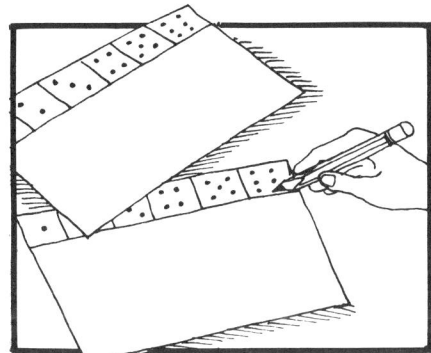

1 Draw six squares at the top of a piece of paper. Put dots on each square to make them look like dice. This makes a score card.

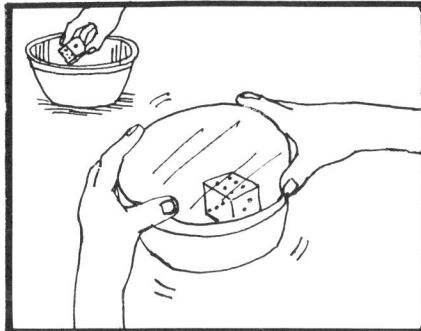

2 Make a score card for each person playing. Put the die in the margarine tub and snap on the lid. Take turns shaking the die and seeing which number comes up.

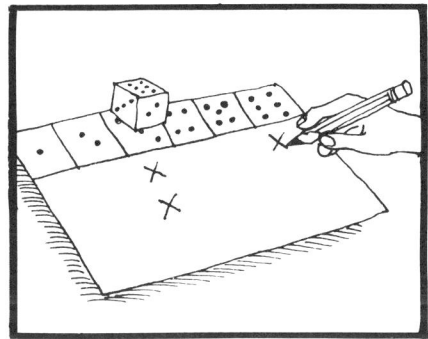

3 After each player shakes, put an x under the square with the matching dot picture on that player's card. The first one who gets four-of-a-kind is the winner.

Try to guess which number is going to come up on the die before you see it.

31

Free Flyer

What you need:

marker
plastic lid from ice cream bucket

What you do:

1 Rinse and dry the lid. Decorate the lid with a pen. Swirls make interesting patterns while the flyer sails.

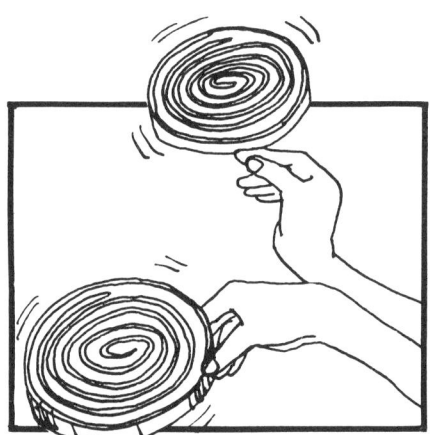

2 Use it for a super quick, super cheap, super fun flyer. Here it comes!

Can you make your flyer land in a cardboard box?

Funny Fences

What you need:

colored plastic spring-type clothespins
an egg carton
paper
scissors
crayons

What you do:

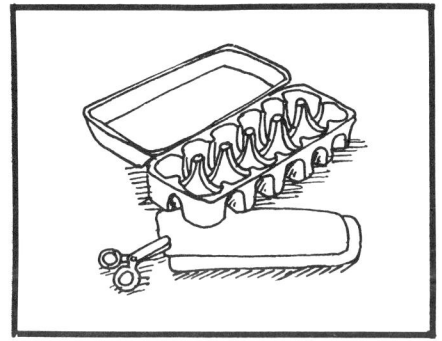

1 Cut the paper in pieces that fit inside the egg carton lid. These are your code cards.

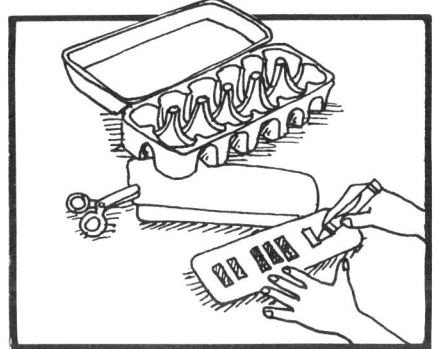

2 Now color your code cards: draw straight lines on pieces of paper with crayons in colors that match the clothespins. Make lots of code cards.

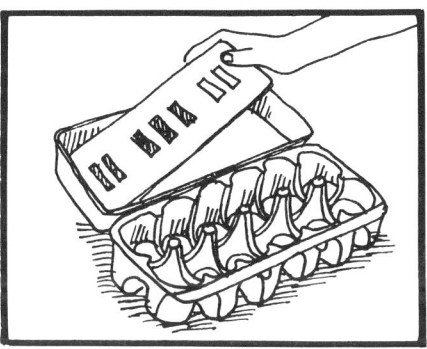

3 Open the egg carton. Put one code card inside the lid so you can see it easily.

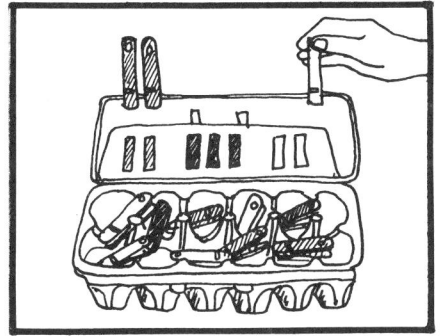

4 Build a fence of clothespins following your code card. If the first line on the card is red, snap a red clothespin on the edge of the egg carton. If the second line is yellow, snap on a yellow one.

5 Go on building your fence till you get to the end of the lines on your code card. Take down your code card and fence and start again with a new card!

If you have a watch, you can time yourself to see how fast you can build a fence and take it down.

33

Giant Grocery Cart

What you need:

empty grocery boxes
large cardboard box
kitchen shears
string
nail
4 plastic lids (same size)
4 brass fasteners

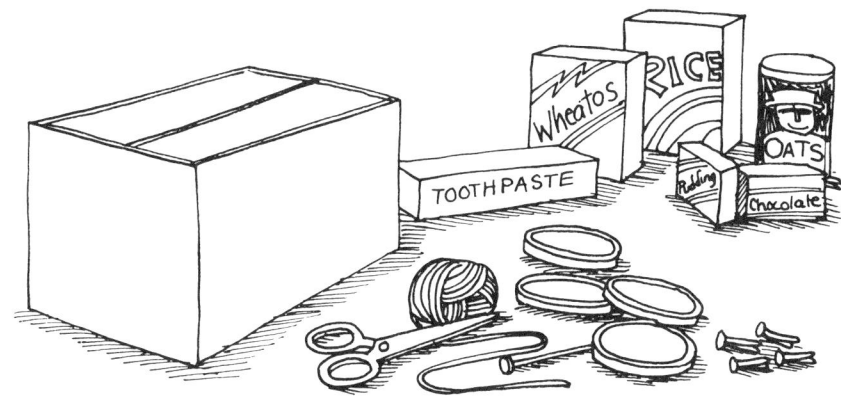

What you do:

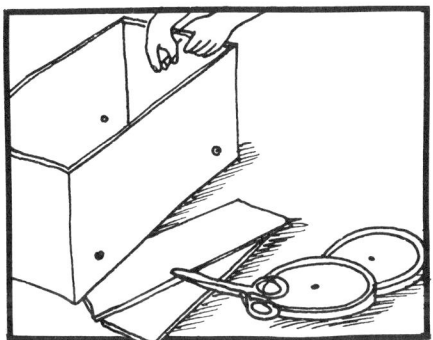

1 Cut the flaps off the box. Punch a hole near the top with the nail. Tie a string to this hole for the grocery cart handle.

2 Punch a center hole in each plastic lid. These are the grocery cart wheels.

3 Punch holes in the box where you want the wheels to go. Fasten the wheels to the box with brass fasteners.

4 Cut flaps off of all the empty food boxes at your house. Then they are easier to play with and you can fit them inside each other. Fill up the cart with your favorite "groceries."

**Got any grocery bags?
You can use them too.**

35

Gone Fishin'

What you need:

paper
scissors
crayon
paper punch
paper clips
pencil
string
magnet
plastic ice cream bucket

What you do:

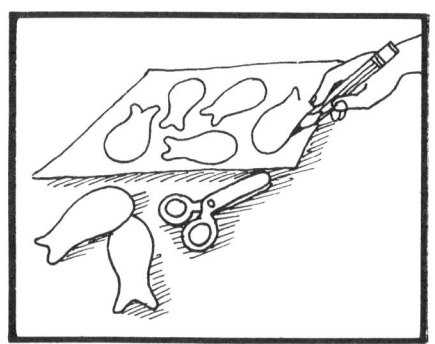

1 Draw lots of fish shapes on paper. Cut out all the fish.

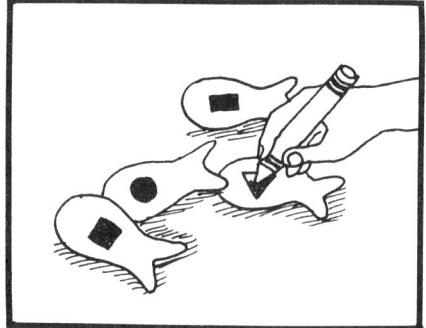

2 Draw a simple shape on each fish: a circle, a triangle, a rectangle or a square.

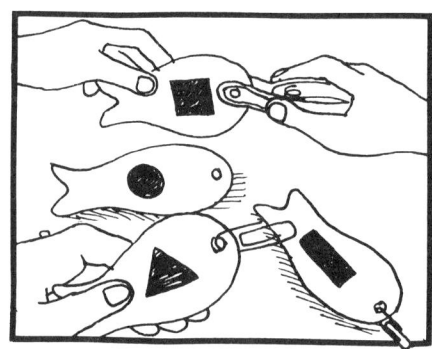

3 Punch a hole in each fish. Then put a paper clip through each hole.

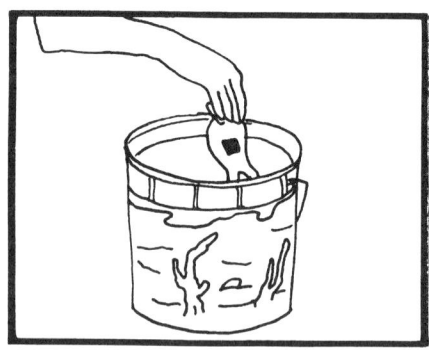

4 Put the fish in the bucket and mix them up.

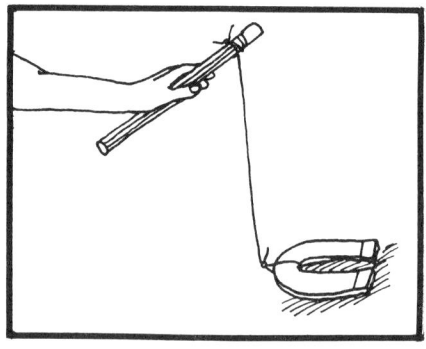

5 Tie the magnet onto the string. Tie the string onto the pencil. This is the fishing pole.

6 Play with friends and each fish for just one shape.

Put your fish back in the "pond" when you're done.

Hat Box

What you need:

hats
cardboard ice cream cartons
 (free from the ice cream store)

What you do:

1 Check garage sales, rummage sales and your own closets for old hats. Try to find as many different hats as you can: baseball cap, straw hat, hardhat, helmet, etc.

2 Put on the hats and pretend to be anyone you want to be. Can you see yourself in a mirror?

3 Store all the hats in cardboard ice cream cartons until the next pretending day comes along.

You can decorate your hat boxes too.

How Long?

What you need:

a tape measure
old magazines
scissors
paste
package of file cards

What you do:

1 Cut out magazine pictures of things you would like to measure.

2 Paste one picture on each file card. Mix up all the cards.

3 Close your eyes and pick a card.

4 Open your eyes. Go and measure that object.

5 Print the length on the card. Keep closing your eyes and picking a card until all the cards are gone, or until you're all measured out!

What's the biggest thing you've found?

Jumpscotch

What you need:

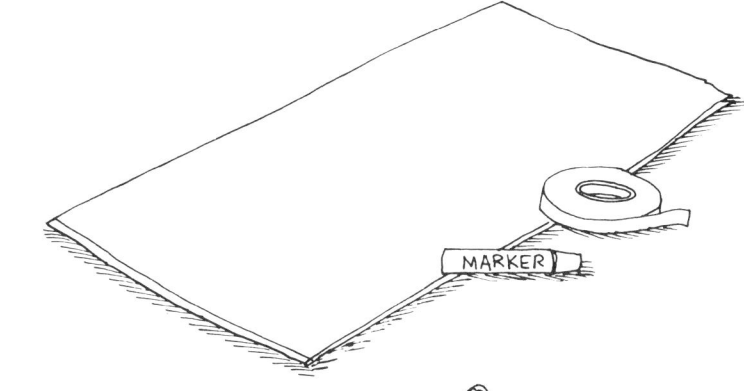

large plastic trash bag
permanent marker
tape

What you do:

1 Lay the trash bag flat on the floor. Use the marker to divide the bag into 7 squares with a big double square (rectangle) at one end. Ask for help if you need it.

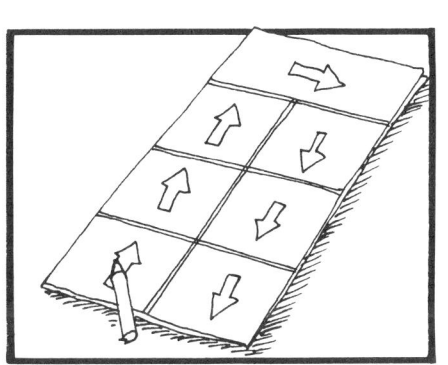

2 Draw arrows going around the bag, with one big arrow in each square.

3 Tape jumpscotch to the floor and play barefoot.

Be sure to tape it so you won't slip.

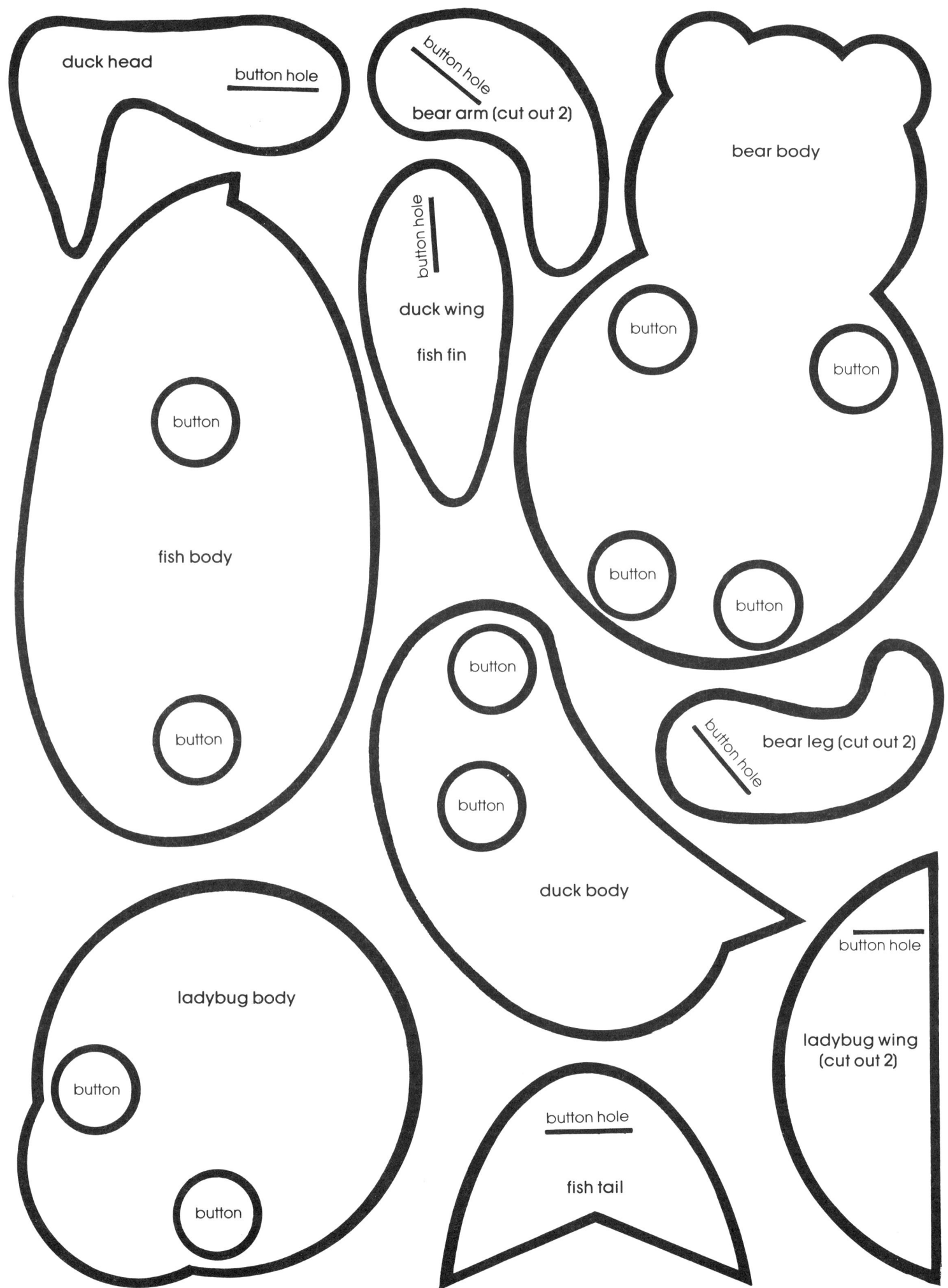

Learn-to-Button Animals

What you need:

animal patterns
tracing paper
felt
pins or tape
ball-point pen
needle
scissors
thread
buttons

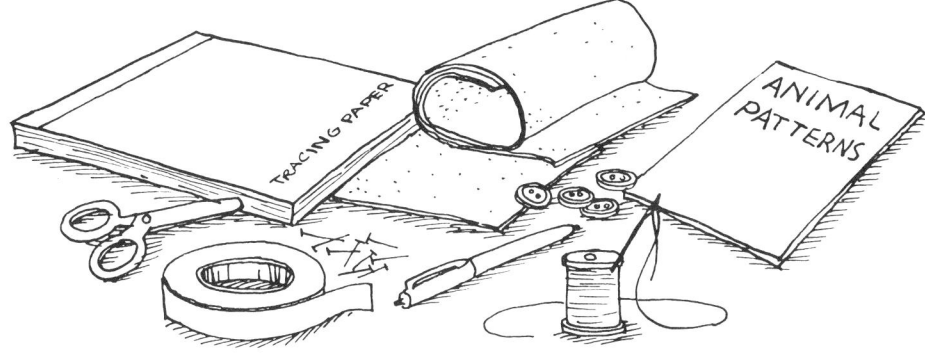

What you do:

1 Put tracing paper over the animal patterns and trace each shape. Cut them out.

2 Lay the shapes on felt. Use a different color felt for each animal. Pin or tape them down. Trace around each shape with a pen.

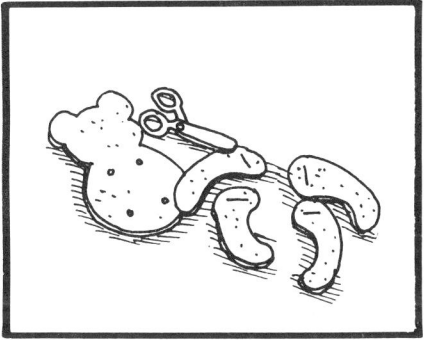

3 Cut the felt shapes out. Cut the button holes in the felt just like they're drawn in the book.

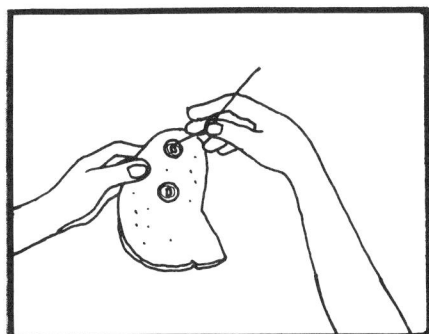

4 Sew buttons on the shapes where they belong.

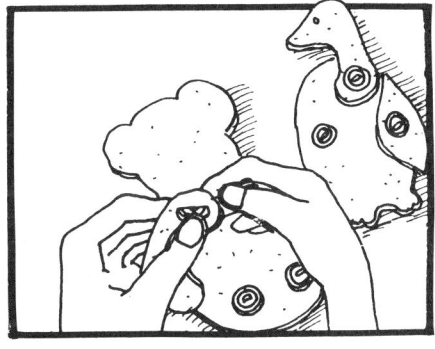

5 Use the animals in three ways: button them together, match colors, and invent crazy, mixed-up animals!

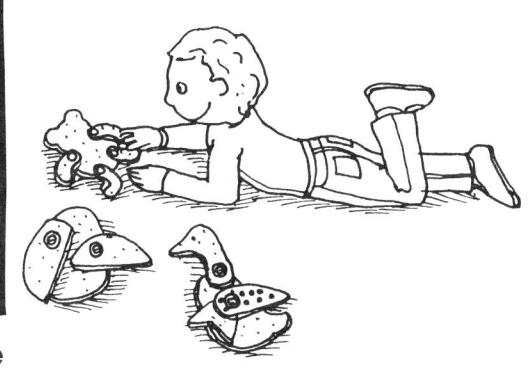

Lid Toss

What you need:

pencil
5 plastic lids (same size)
scissors
cardboard tube from paper towels
margarine tub

What you do:

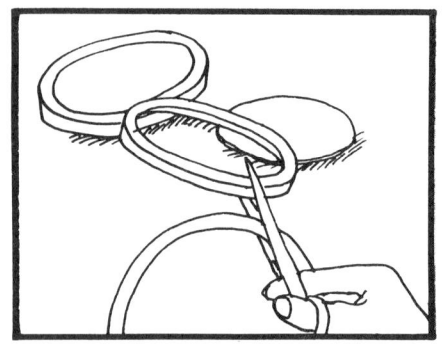

1 Cut the centers from the plastic lids. Save the rings.

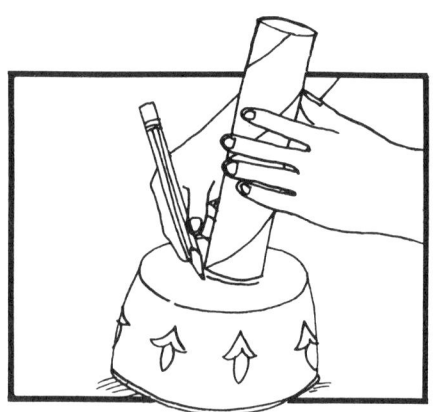

2 Trace the circle of the cardboard tube on the bottom of the margarine tub. Now cut the circle out.

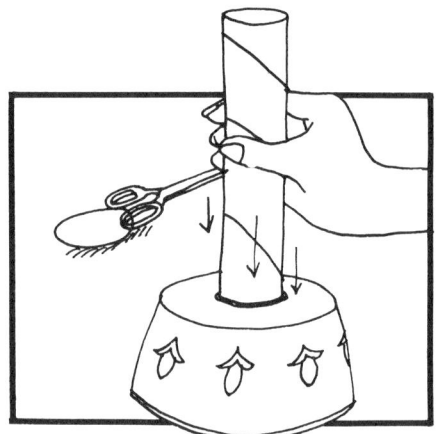

3 Turn the margarine tub upside down. Push the tube into the hole.

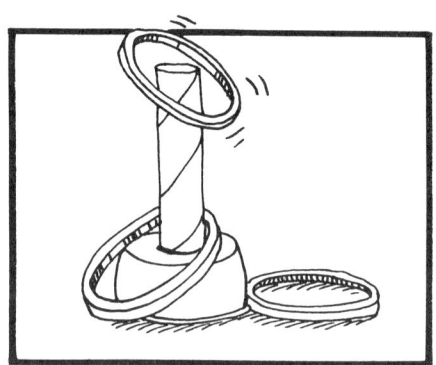

4 Toss the rings over the tube, scoring one point for each good throw. This is a fun game to play with a friend.

As you get better you can toss your rings from farther and farther away.

Little Bubbles

What you need:

spring-type clothespin
spice-bottle top (the kind with the holes)
liquid detergent
margarine tub

What you do:

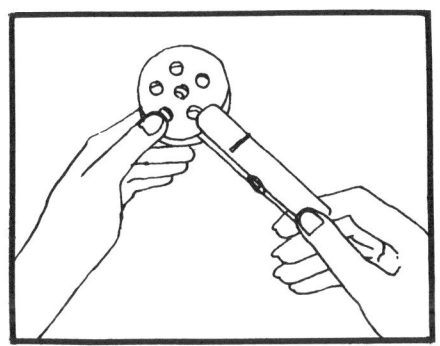

1 Clip the clothespin onto the spice-bottle top.

2 Pour some detergent into a margarine tub and dip in the top.

3 Hold the clothespin handle and blow through the holes in the bottle top. You'll get bubbles galore!

Be nice and make a second bubble blower for a friend. Wanna have a bubble blowing contest?

Lunchbox

What you need:

old magazines
scissors
paste
file cards
old lunchbox

What you do:

1 Cut out lots of magazine pictures. Cut some of food and some of objects.

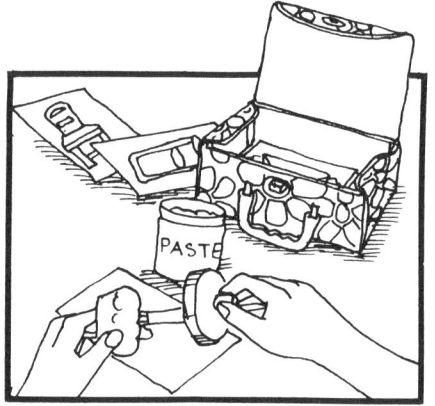

2 Paste the pictures onto file cards. Make sure that the cards will fit into the lunchbox.

3 Mix up the cards. Sort the pictures. Only the food pictures go into the lunchbox! No lunchbox? Use a lunch bag and you're all set to play.

Pack a snack and a lunch for tomorrow.

Macaroni Match

What you need:

2 kinds of noodles that can be strung
shoelace
bowl
file cards
pencil

What you do:

1 Put the macaroni in a bowl and mix well. Knot the shoelace at one end.

2 Use pencil to draw pictures of different patterns of macaroni on file cards. Show the stringing pattern, such as 2 straight noodles, 3 round ones, 2 straight. These are code cards. Make lots of them.

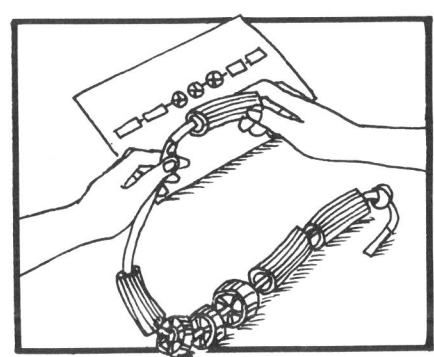

3 Using one card at a time, follow the codes and string away.

Tie the ends of your nicest string of macaroni-beads together and you've got a necklace or bracelet.

Magazine Picture Dictionary

What you need:

paper
yarn or string
pencil
old magazines
scissors
paste

What you do:

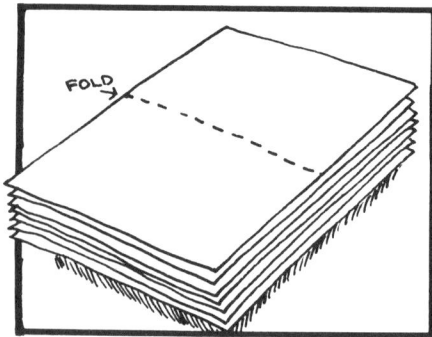

1 Stack 7 pieces of paper about the size of this book in a neat pile. Fold the pile in half.

2 Tie a string or piece of yarn at the fold so you make a book with a front and back cover. Decorate the covers if you'd like.

3 Print a capital and small A at the top of the first page (the inside of the front cover) and go on through the book with the rest of the alphabet.

4 Find a picture in a magazine of something that begins with each letter of the alphabet.

5 Paste each picture on the page that has its starting letter.

6 Then "read" your alphabet book beginning with "A is for ____ , B is for ____ ." Read it again to someone else.

What a wonderful book you've made!

Marble Track

What you need:

cardboard tubes from paper towels
scissors
glue
paper punch
string
marbles

What you do:

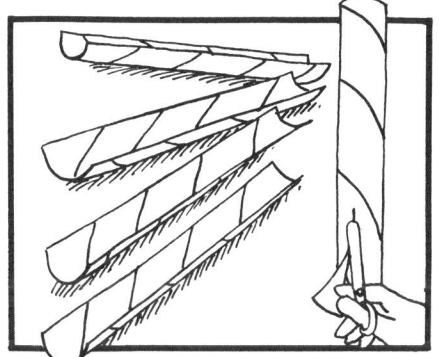

1 Cut the cardboard tubes in half LENGTHWISE.

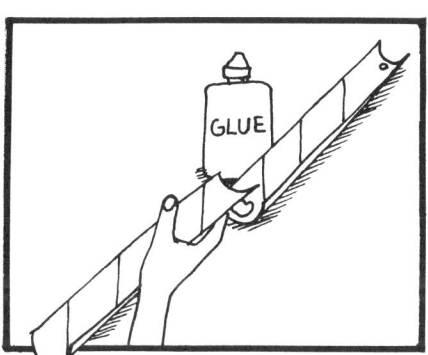

2 Glue the tubes together at ends to form a long track.

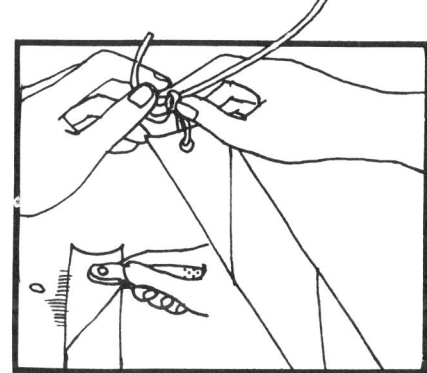

3 Punch a hole at one end of the track. Tie a string handle to the hole.

4 Hook the track onto a door knob and roll marbles down. Whee!

Try aiming your marbles at a target like a tipped-over ice cream bucket or margarine tub. Can you make them hit the target and stay inside?

Moon People

What you need:

spring-type clothespins
L'eggs stockings egg
permanent marker

What you do:

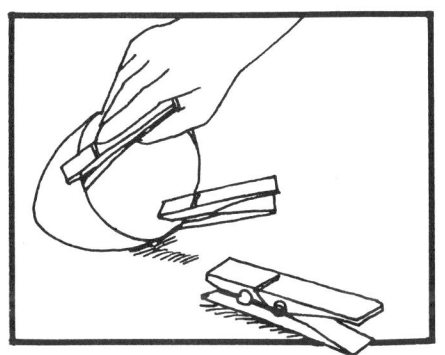

1 Snap 3 spring-type clothespins onto half of a L'eggs stockings egg. Repeat with the other egg half.

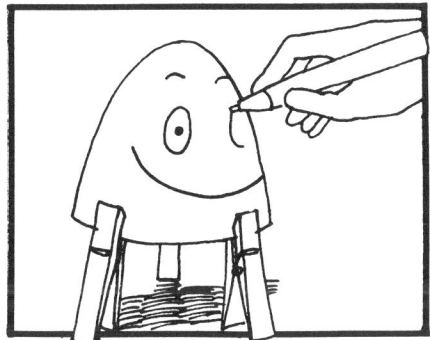

2 Add faces with permanent marker.

3 Your Moon People are ready for exploring and you're the guide!

What kinds of sounds do moon people make?

Musical Door Hook

What you need:

large metal door hook
shoelace
nail

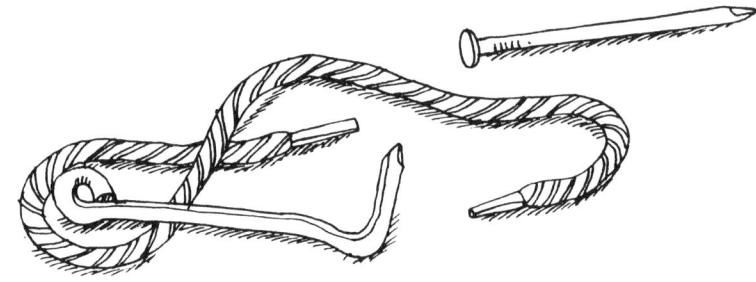

What you do:

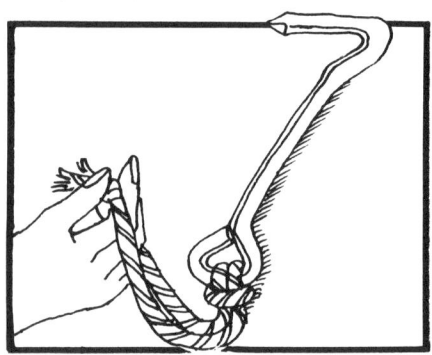

1 Buy the biggest metal door hook you can find at a hardware store. Tie the shoelace onto the hook.

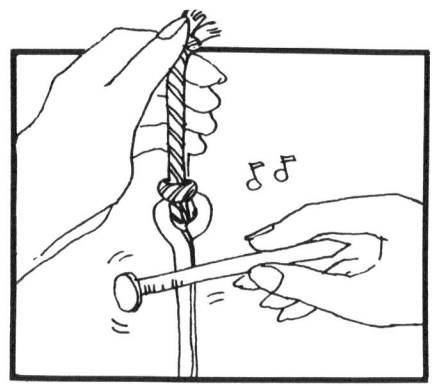

2 Hit the hook with the nail. Isn't that a pretty sound? Your musical door hook doesn't look like a triangle but it sure rings like one! Cheaper too.

What else makes music?

My Book

What you need:

- paper
- string
- old magazines
- scissors
- paste
- pencil

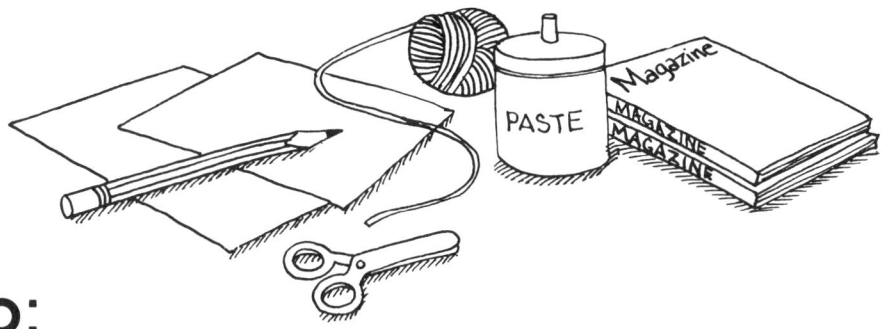

What you do:

1 Stack several pieces of paper the size of this book in a neat pile. Fold the pile in half.

2 Tie a string or piece of yarn at the fold so you make a book with a front and back cover. Draw pictures of yourself on the covers.

3 Cut out magazine pictures that tell something about you: food you like to eat or toys you like to play with.

4 Paste a picture on each page of the book. Print a story about yourself beneath each picture or ask someone to print it for you.

That's a special book!

Name Worm

What you need:

paper
pencil
scissors

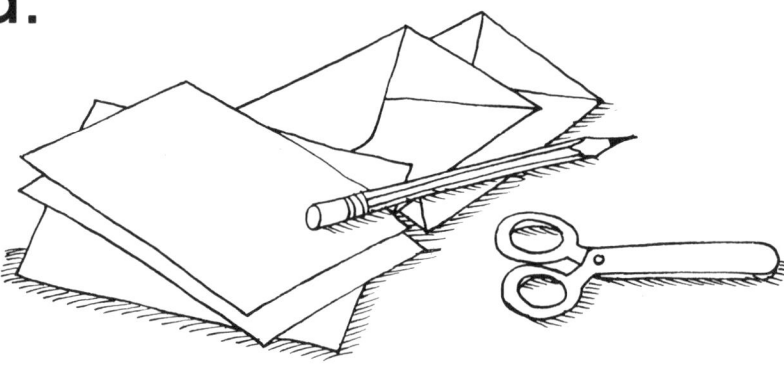

What you do:

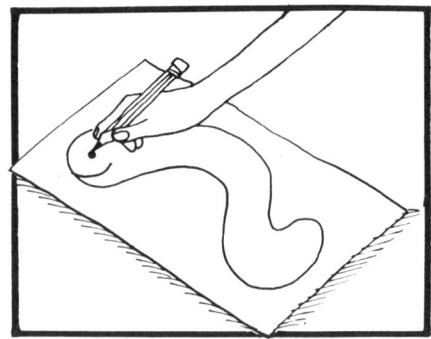

1 Draw a fat, wiggly worm shape on paper. Put a dot at the left for an eye, as in the picture.

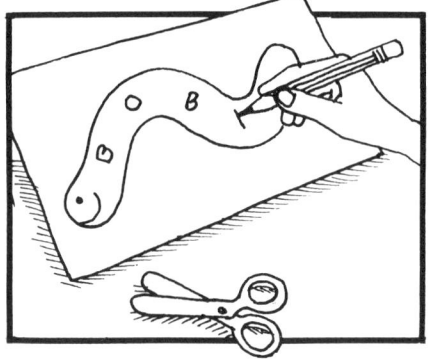

2 Print your name on the worm, leaving a space between each letter.

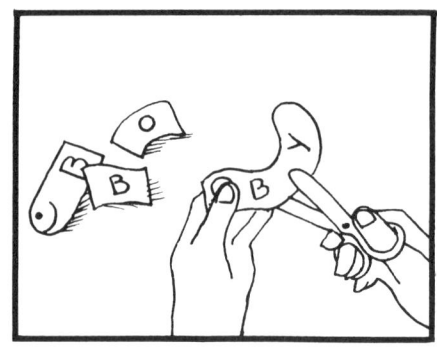

3 Cut the worm into puzzle pieces.

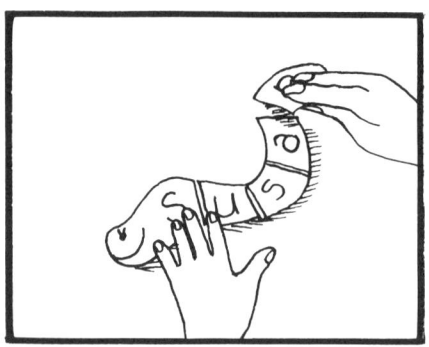

4 Put your name worm puzzle back together.

5 Lots of name worm puzzles could be made from colored paper, one color for each name. Store them all in a can for your "bucket of worms."

Can you scramble the names and make up new ones?

Nothing-to-Do Cards

What you need:

package of file cards
pencil
paper punch
yarn or string

What you do:

1 Think of lots of things you like to do, such as looking at books, baking cookies, watering plants and building with blocks.

2 Punch a hole in each card. Print one idea on each file card.

3 Tie all the cards together. Save the cards for a day when you've got the "bluckies."

4 Close your eyes and pick a card. You've found something super to do!

You can make a second set of cards on another day too.

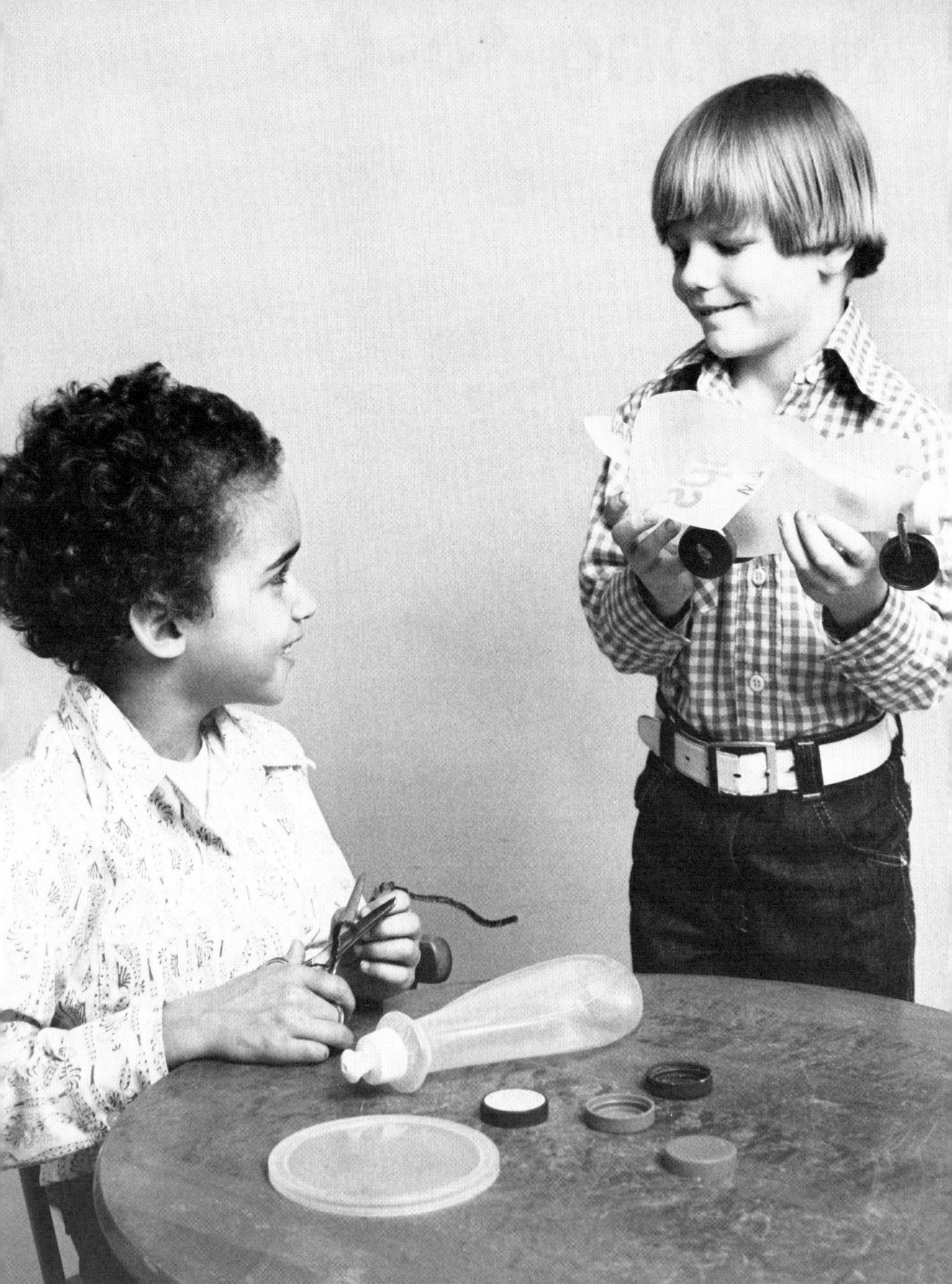

Plain Plane

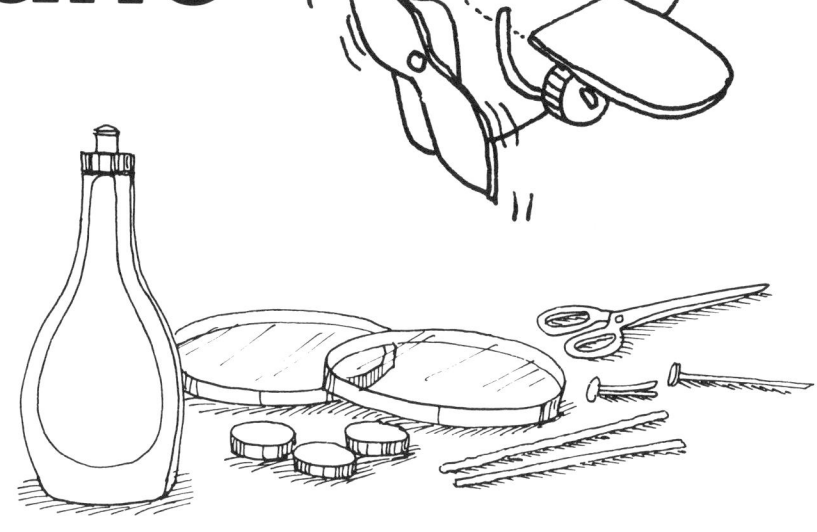

What you need:

plastic detergent bottle with top
kitchen shears
3 plastic bottle tops (same size)
2 pipe cleaners
large plastic lids
1 brass fastener

What you do:

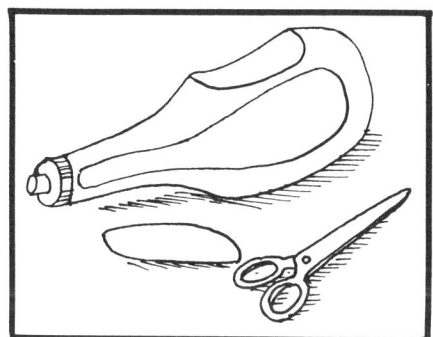

1 Rinse and dry the detergent bottle, then screw on the top. Cut a hole in one side of the bottle. This is the cockpit.

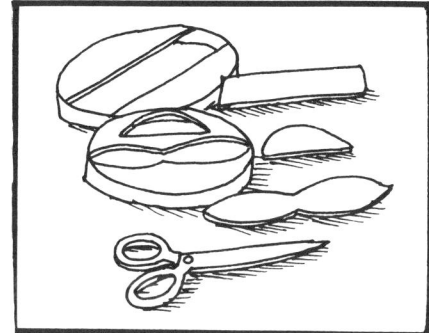

2 Cut any shape propeller, wing and tail from plastic lids.

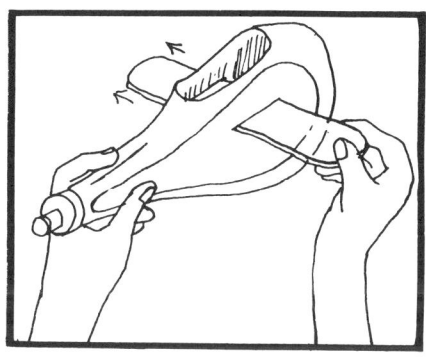

3 Carefully cut two slits beneath cockpit hole, one on each side of the plane. Push the wing through these slits, forming cockpit seat. Fasten tail to back in same way.

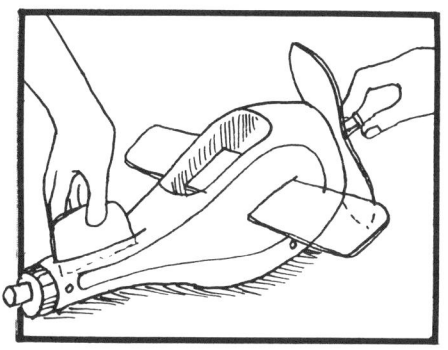

4 Poke a hole in center of the propeller.
Poke a matching hole in front of plane with nail. Fasten propeller to plane with brass fastener.

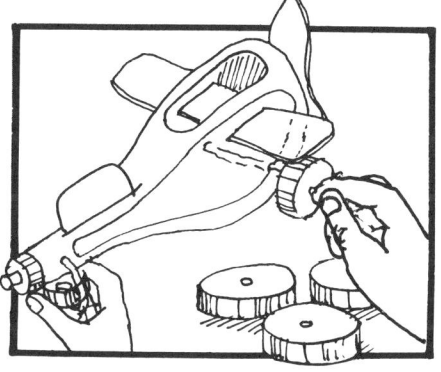

5 Poke holes in bottle where you want the wheels to go. Fasten wheels with pipe cleaners, pushing them through the bottle and bending ends so wheels won't fall off.

Play Stove

What you need:
small box (such as a shoebox)
paper
scissors
glue
2 plastic lids
2 brass fasteners
nail

What you do:

1 Cut some circles from paper.

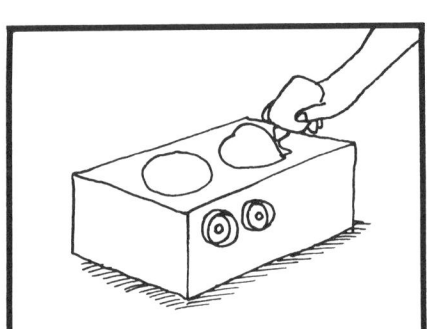

2 Glue the circles onto the bottom of the upside down box. These are the stove burners.

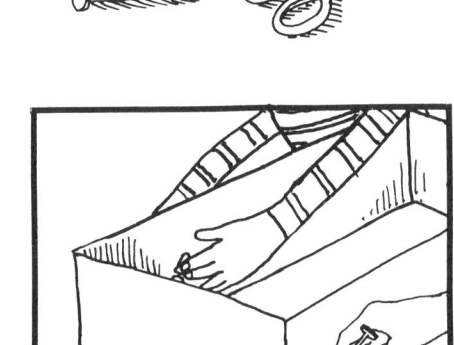

3 Use the nail to poke holes in the center of the plastic lids. Attach the lids to the box with brass fasteners. These are the stove knobs.

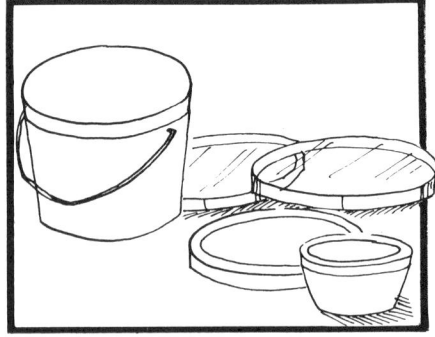

4 Pans can be anything you have around; margarine tubs, plastic scoops, plastic bottle tops. Soup's on!

Be sure the stove's off when you're done.

56

Playday Playclay

What you need:

plastic ice cream bucket with lid
flour
water
salt
measuring cup
food coloring
permanent marker
household stuff

What you do:

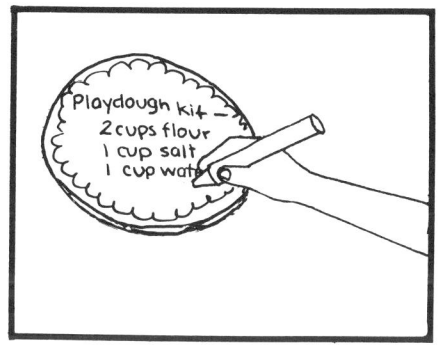

1 Use the marker to print the playdough recipe on the bucket so it's always handy.

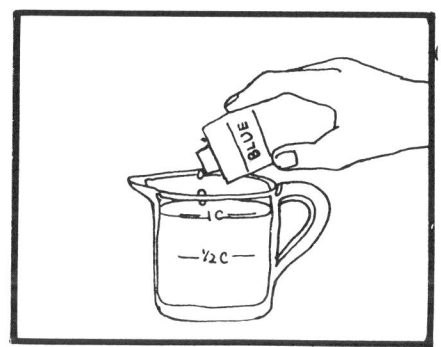

2 Add a few drops of food coloring to a cup of water.

3 Make dough from 2 cups flour, 1 cup water, and 1 cup salt. Mush and squish the playclay for about 10 minutes.

4 Use safe stuff from around your house with your playclay: margarine tubs, spools, popsicle sticks, plastic animals, cookie cutters.

5 Keep the playclay inside the ice cream bucket.

What's cookin'?

57

Playhouse

What you need:

giant cardboard box
knife
marking pens

What you do:

1 Cut a door and some windows in the sides of the box. Tape the flaps together to make a roof.

2 Decorate your box. You could add shutters, doorknobs, shingles, floors, walls, wallpaper, pictures and an attic.

3 Smaller boxes and containers make good tables.

Move in and play the day away.

Rainbow Book

What you need:

colored paper
string
old magazines
scissors
paste

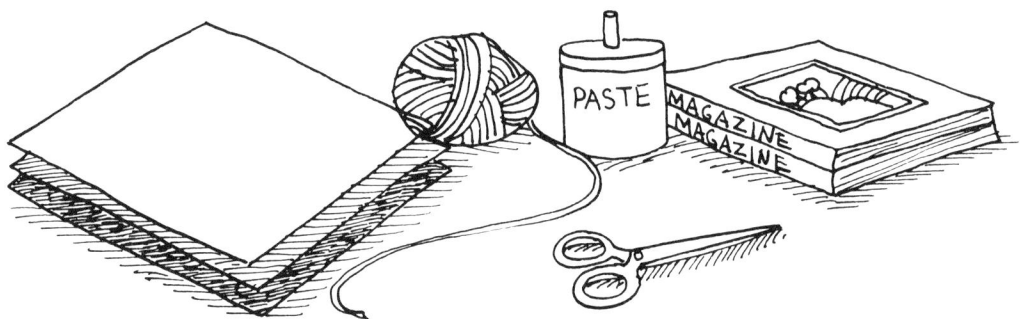

What you do:

1 Stack several pieces of colored paper about the size of this book in a neat pile. Fold the pile in half.

2 Tie a string or piece of yarn at the fold so you make a book.

3 Cut out magazine pictures. Look for lots of different colors.

4 Paste the pictures on the matching colored paper page.

5 Look at that rainbow of colors! Have you ever seen a rainbow?

6 Now make up a story about your colorful pictures.

What's your favorite color?

Rhymers

What you need:

egg carton
ball-point pen
button

What you do:

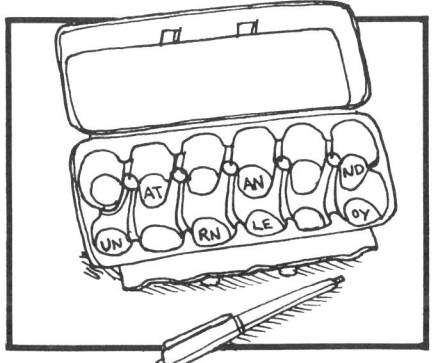

1 Print word endings in some of the bumps in the bottom of the egg carton: __ at, __ an, __ un.

2 In the blank spaces draw a smiling face.

3 Put the button in the egg carton and close the lid. Shake the carton and open the lid.

4 If the button lands on an ending, think of as many words as you can that rhyme with that ending.

5 If the button lands on a smiling face, clap for yourself. You're terrific!

You can use beginnings of words in another egg carton: two letters like "sh," "br" and "th" are good starts.

Ring-O

What you need:

plastic lid
scissors
cardboard tube from paper towels
paper punch
string

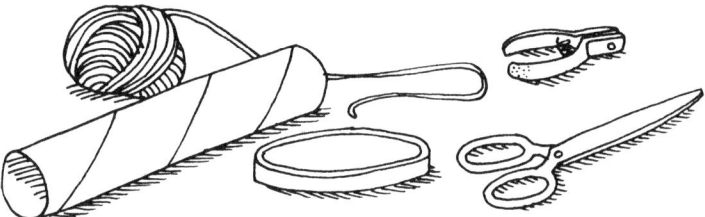

What you do:

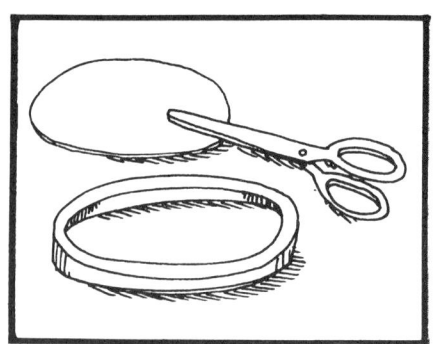
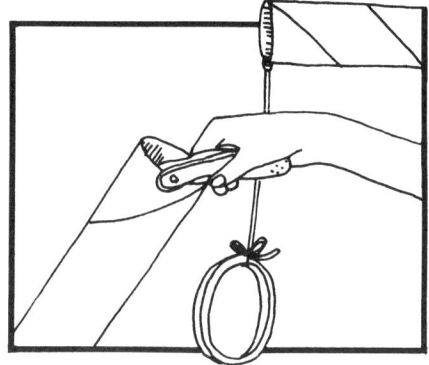
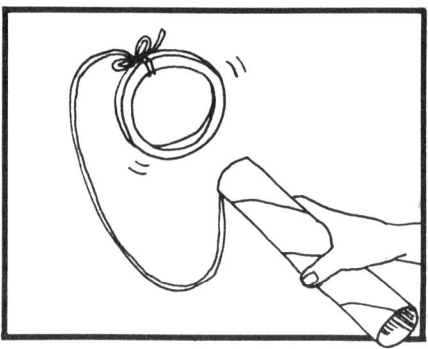

1 Leaving a rim, cut out the inside from the plastic lid. This makes a ring.

2 Punch a hole at one end of the cardboard tube. Tie the plastic ring onto the tube with a 12" string.

3 Slowly swing the ring and catch it on the tube. Please don't catch a lamp!

Can you catch the ring with your eyes closed?

Sand Pendulum

What you need:

plastic detergent bottle
kitchen shears
paper punch
string
sand or uncooked rice

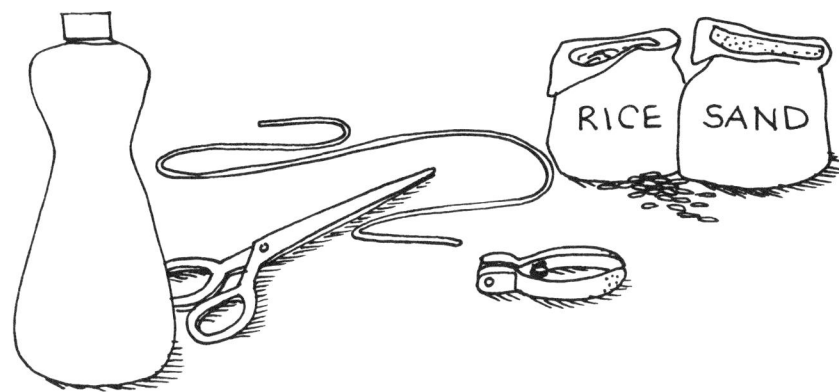

What you do:

1 Cut the tapered top off the detergent bottle.

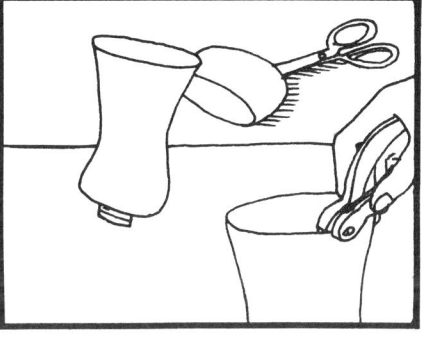

2 Punch two holes on the cut edge of the top. Make the holes opposite each other.

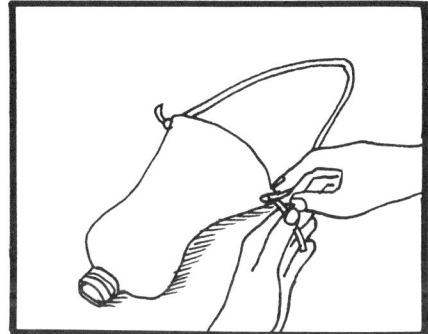

3 Cut a string to use for a handle.
Tie the string through the holes.

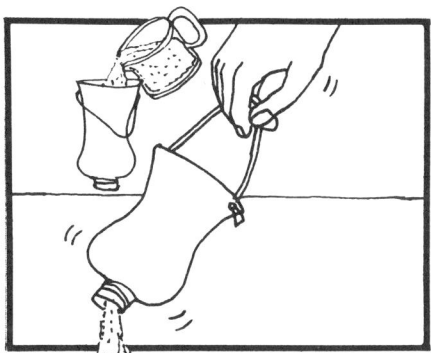

4 Fill your pendulum with sand, or dry, uncooked rice and swing it.

Also nice with rice: scoops, plastic cups and bottles.

Shadow Puppets

What you need:

cookie cutters
pencil
paper
scissors
paper punch
glue
popsicle sticks

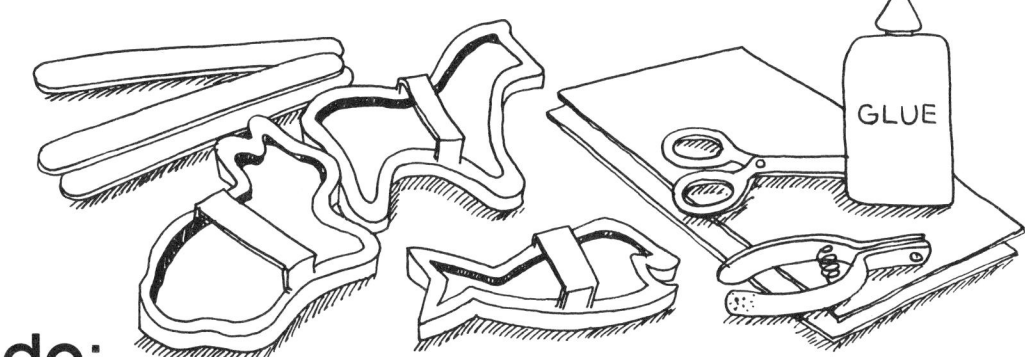

What you do:

1 Using the cookie cutters as patterns, trace around them on paper.

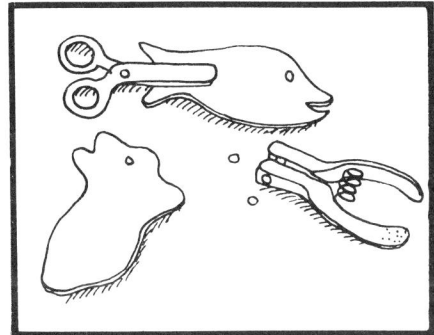

2 Cut out the paper cookies. Punch eyes where needed with paper punch.

3 Glue shapes onto popsicle sticks.

4 Enjoy your shadow puppets indoors with a flashlight or outdoors in the sun.

Make up stories and act them out with your puppets.

Shape Sorting

What you need:

coffee can with plastic lid
scissors
ball-point pen
tops from plastic milk bottles
large sponge
clothespins

What you do:

1 Rinse and dry the bottle tops. Then cut the sponge into squares.

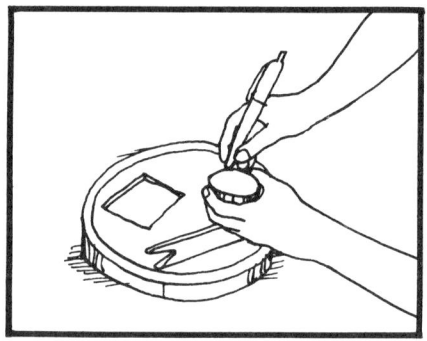

2 Use the pen to trace a clothespin, a sponge square and a bottle top on the coffee can lid.

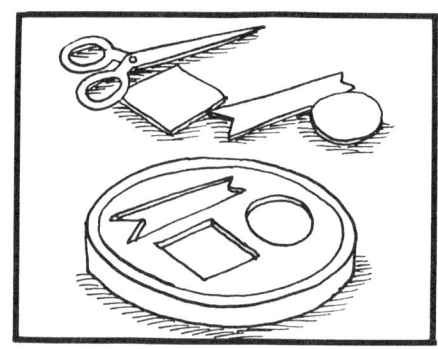

3 Cut the shapes out from the lid.

4 Push all objects through their matching holes. Keep all game parts right in the can.

How fast can you sort out all those shapes?

Silly Eggs

What you need:

L'eggs stockings eggs
paper
crayons
scissors

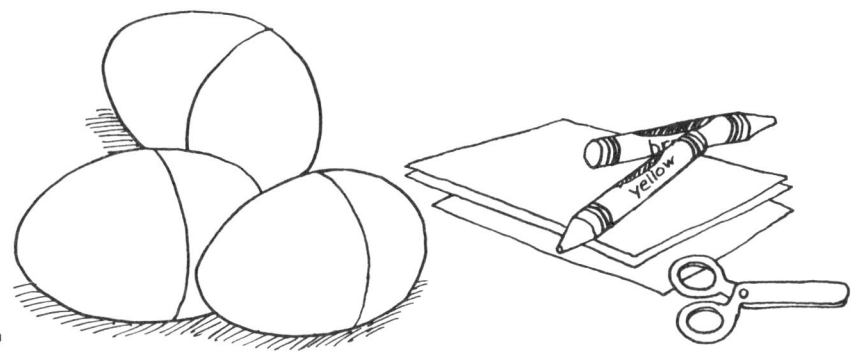

What you do:

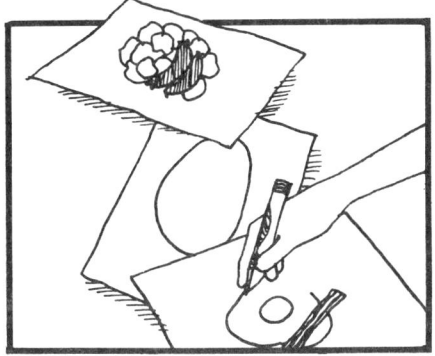

1 Draw egg pictures on paper with crayons: one picture of scrambled eggs, one of fried eggs, one of bacon and eggs, one of boiled eggs.

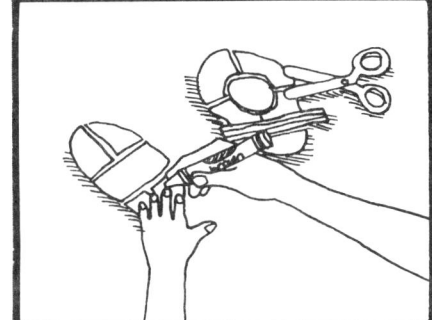

2 Cut one picture into puzzle pieces.

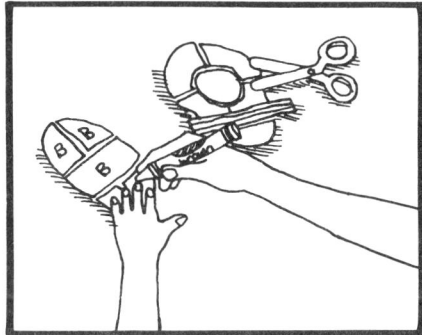

3 Code all the pieces of that puzzle so they won't get mixed up. Put a "B" on the backs of the pieces of the boiled egg picture, or an "F" on the fried, etc. Then cut and code the other pictures.

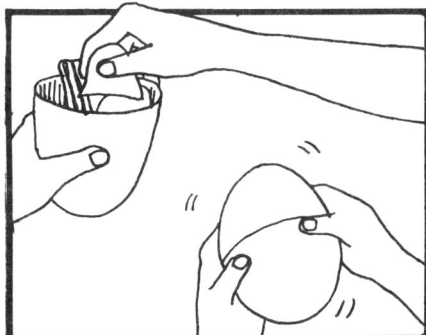

4 Put a puzzle inside each egg. Shake. Which one do you want to do first?

You can shape your silly eggs with your friends too.

Space Helmet

What you need:

large cardboard ice cream carton (free from the ice cream store)
kitchen shears
marker
nail
pipe cleaner

What you do:

1 Rinse and dry the ice cream carton. Turn it upside down. Cut out openings (eye holes, etc.).

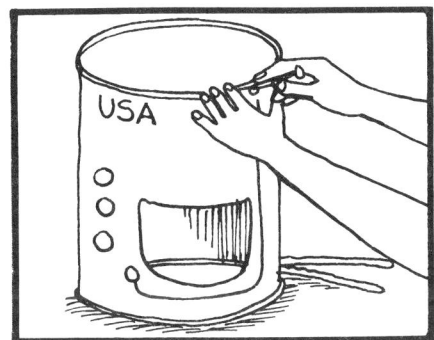

2 Draw some wires and knobs with a marker. Poke two holes next to each other near the top of the carton.

3 Push the pipe cleaner through the holes. Twist so it won't fall off. This is your antenna. Put your space helmet on and take a walk on the beautiful planet earth!

Watch your step as you explore!

69

Spongy Blocks

What you need:

cheap sponges
a plastic bucket

What you do:

1 Buy a bag of the cheapest sponges you can find. Store them in an empty bucket.

2 Build bridges and drive cars under them.

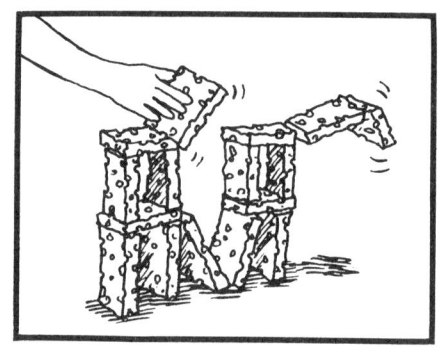

3 Build buildings. When you knock them down, they crash without a sound, like a silent movie.

Can you blow down a tower with one puff?

Stars-in-the-Moon Mobile

What you need:

wire coat hanger
plastic lids
kitchen shears
paper punch
string

What you do:

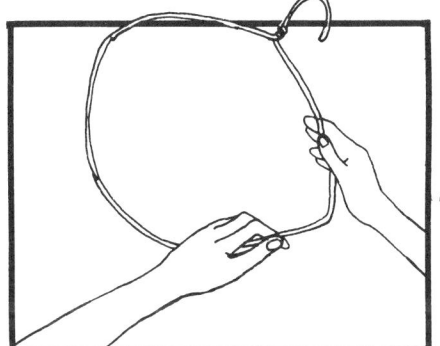

1 Bend the coat hanger into a circle. This is the moon.

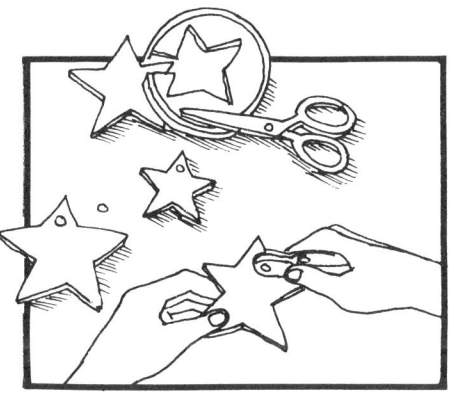

2 Cut different-sized stars from plastic lids. Punch a hole in each star.

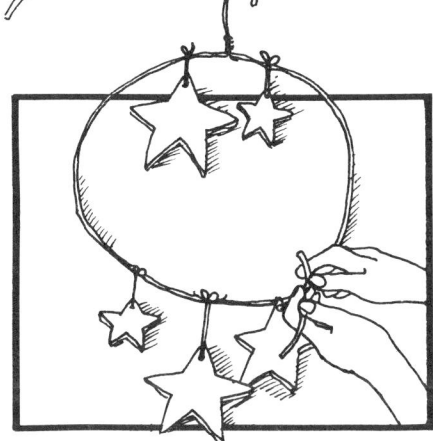

3 Tie the stars onto the hanger with string. How many stars are shining over you?

If you hang your mobile somewhere where a breeze can hit it, your stars will dance.

Stickeroo

What you need:

shallow box with lid
flannel
felt
scissors
glue

What you do:

1 Trace around the box lid and cut a rectangle from flannel the same size as the box lid.

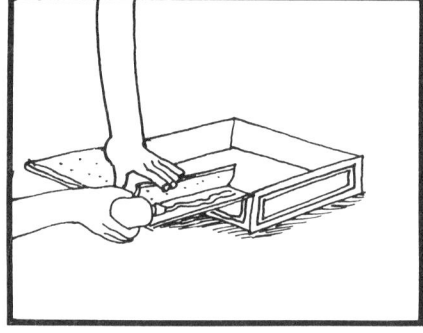

2 Glue the rectangle inside the lid.

3 Cut all kinds of shapes from felt: circles, ovals, squares, triangles, rectangles and "wiggle-wobbles."

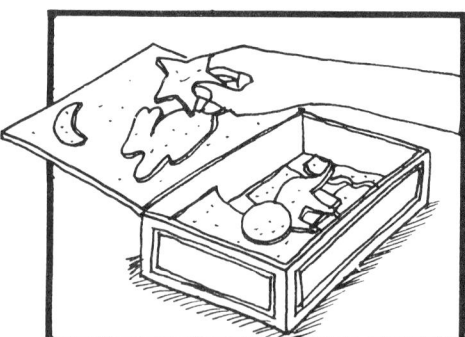

4 Make pictures by pressing the shapes to the flannel.

Gee, you make pretty pictures.

Stitcheroo

What you need:

Styrofoam meat trays
nail
pencil or pen
long shoelace

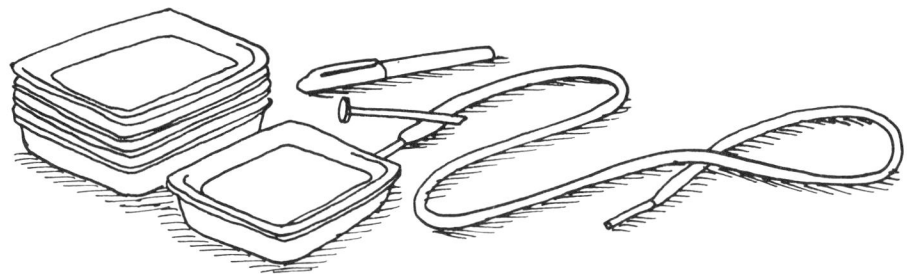

What you do:

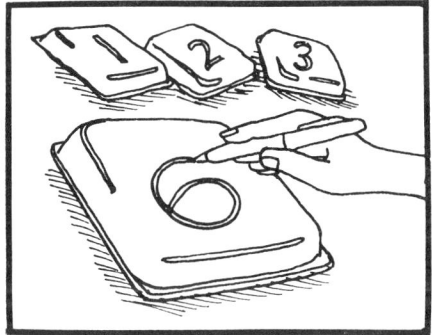

1 Rinse and dry the Styrofoam meat trays. Print a number on each meat tray, going from 1 to 10. Make them big!

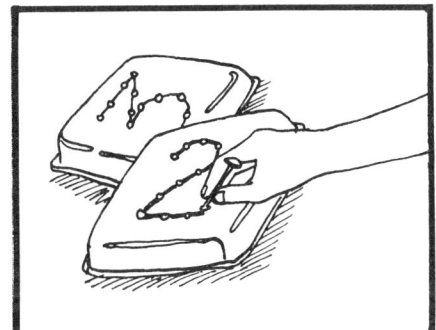

2 Poke some holes along each number with the nail. Leave space between holes.

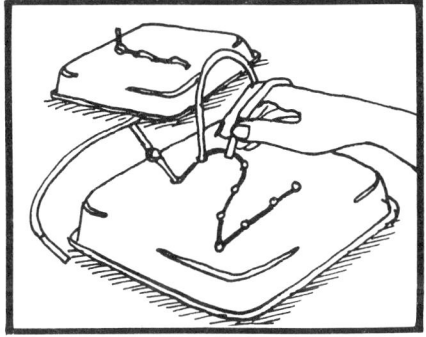

3 Knot one end of the shoelace so it doesn't pull out. Stitch along each number card. You sure can do stitcheroo!

Can you make sticheroo letters for your name?

Stop Light

What you need:

yardstick
coffee can with plastic lid
sand, gravel or stones
red, yellow, green paper
scissors
glue

What you do:

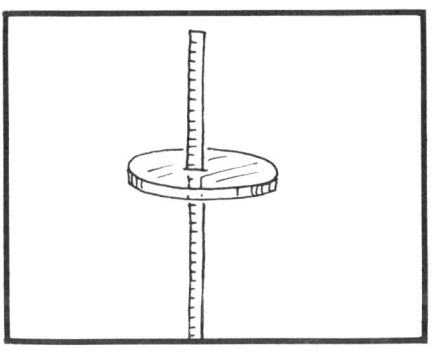

1 Cut a small slit in the plastic coffee can lid to fit the top of the yardstick. Slip the yardstick through the slit.

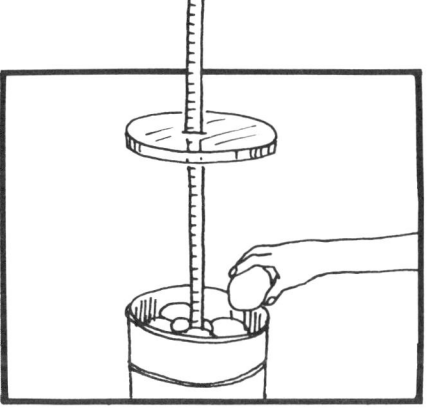

2 Put stones or something in the bottom of the can so it doesn't tip over. Snap on the can lid.

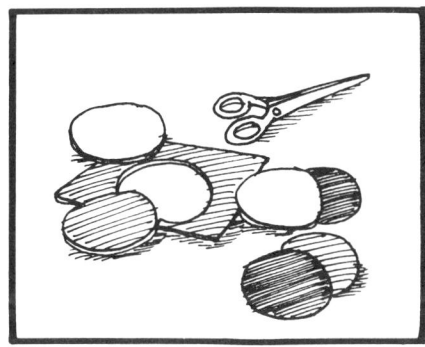

3 Cut 2 red, 2 yellow and 2 green circles from paper. Make them all the same size. Glue the circles onto the top of the yardstick.

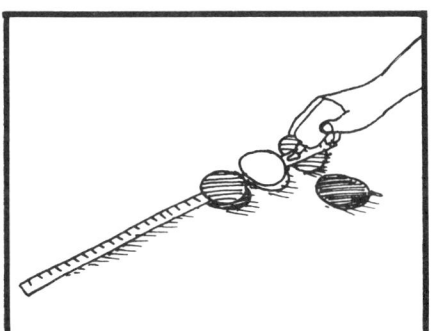

4 On one side glue red at the top, yellow in the middle, and green below. On the other side glue green at the top, then yellow, and then red. That way the stop light can "change" when you turn the yardstick around.

Use the stop light with bikes.

75

Story Spinner

What you need:

scissors
paste
old magazines
nail
1 brass fastener
diaper pin or large paper clip
cardboard pizza tray (from frozen pizza)

What you do:

1 Cut out a bunch of magazine pictures.

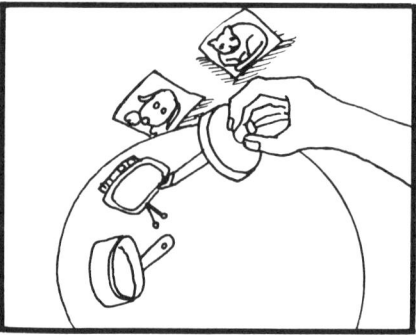

2 Paste them around the pizza tray.

3 Punch a hole in the center of the circle with the nail.

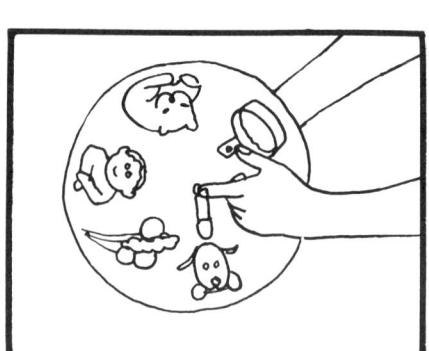

4 Fasten a diaper pin or large paper clip to the hole with the brass fastener. This is the game spinner.

5 Spin the spinner and tell a story including each picture it points to — don't worry if you get the same picture several times. Just continue the story.

6 You can make a second story spinner on the other side of the cardboard pizza tray. Tell some silly stories; the sillier the better!

Super Scoop

What you need:

laundry detergent bottle with handle
kitchen shears

What you do:

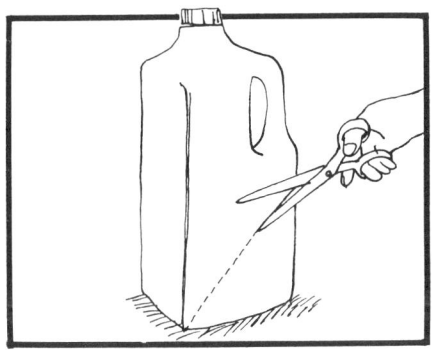

1 Cut the bottom off the bottle.

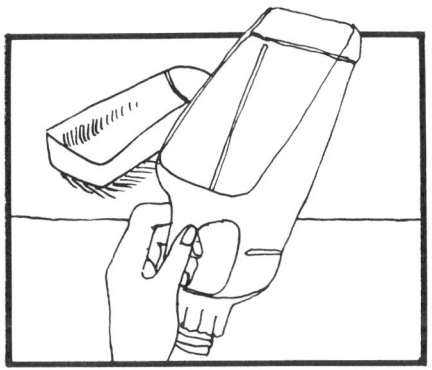

2 Leave the handle alone, but cut two sides from the bottle. Slant these cuts so you form a scoop.

3 Use your scoop to dig, to scoop and to pour sand or snow out the open top. Gee, that's fun!

Scoop out tunnels, pile up mountains and make lakes.

77

Target Toss

What you need:
large magazine or newspaper picture
paste
cardboard
marker
something to throw
 (ball, sponge, plastic pot-scrubber, knotted sock)

What you do:

1 Cut out a large picture from a magazine or newspaper. Paste the picture onto cardboard. This is the target.

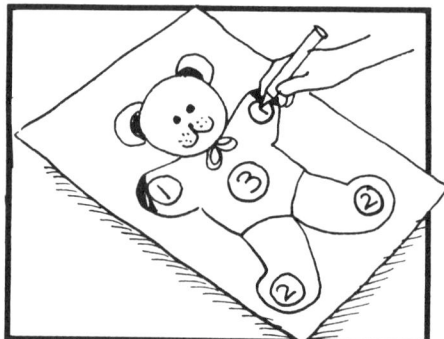

2 Use marker to print numbers on different parts of the target. These tell the points scored.

3 Take turns throwing the ball at the target. The one with the highest score wins.

Once you can hit the target easily, try throwing from even farther back.

Terrific Target

What you need:

something to throw
  (ball, sponge, plastic pot-scrubber, knotted sock)
plastic lid
garbage bag tie (the jaggedy kind)
nail

What you do:

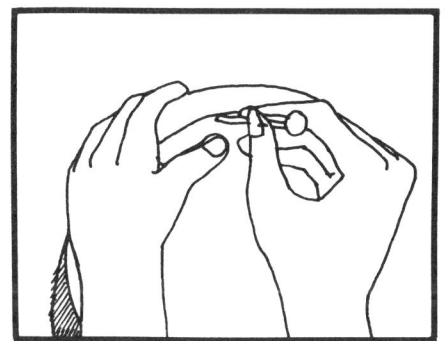

1 Poke a hole near the edge of the lid with the nail.

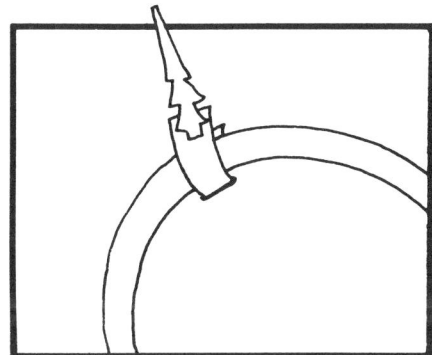

2 Push the garbage bag tie through the hole.

3 Hang the target anywhere. Throw a ball, plastic pot-scrubber, sponge, knotted sock, or snowball at the target. Water pistols work well outside too.

Ready? Aim! Fire! When you can hit the target five times in a row, you're ready for smaller targets. Targets can also be decorated.

Tic-tac Tops

What you need:

10 plastic milk bottle tops
a permanent marker
paper

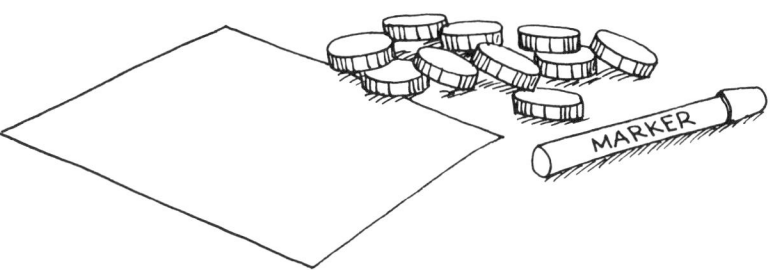

What you do:

1 Gather 10 plastic tops from plastic milk bottles.

2 Make x's on 5 of the tops and o's on 5 of the tops.

3 Draw tic-tac-toe lines on paper and you're ready to play.

You can have a contest with a friend and see who can win 3 games out of 5, or 5 games out of 7.

Toothpaste

What you need:

magazine picture of toothpaste
magazine picture of a toothbrush
scissors
paste
package of file cards
marking pen

What you do:

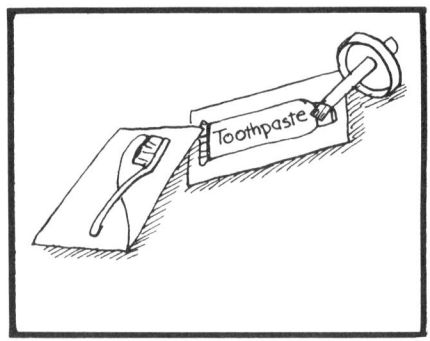

1 Cut out the magazine pictures. Paste them onto file cards. Now you have a toothpaste card and a toothbrush card.

2 Use the marking pen to draw lines on blank file cards. Always start at one edge of a card and end at another edge. Make all sorts of lines.

3 Lay the toothpaste card on the floor. Then lay the line cards down on the floor, connecting the lines in any way you want, to show the path the toothpaste takes.

4 Finally, lay down the toothbrush card at the end of the toothpaste path. The toothpaste always gets to the brush!

Whose teeth are you going to brush now?

Vegetable Soup

What you need:

small saucepan
paper
pencil
old magazines
scissors
paste

What you do:

1 Trace around the bottom of the saucepan on paper. Make lots of these circles. Cut out all the circles.

2 Cut out magazine pictures of all kinds of food.

3 Paste each food picture on a paper circle and mix them up.

4 To make "vegetable soup," sort pictures of vegetables into the pan.

Did you put chocolate cake in your vegetable soup?

Wash-Me Mit

What you need:

an old washcloth
scissors
needle
thread
yarn
permanent marker

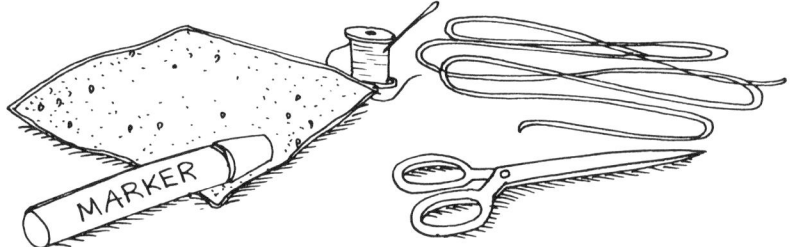

What you do:

1 Cut the washcloth in half. Fold that half in half. Stitch around two open sides of cloth, curving up toward the folded top.

2 Loop yarn fringe along the folded top of your wash-me mit if you want it to have hair. Stitch it in place.

3 Draw a face on the mit with a marker. Repeat the whole business with the other half washcloth to make a second mit.

Hmmmm. Two mits for two hands. You'll be the cleanest kid in town!

Washing Machine

What you need:

large cardboard ice cream carton (free from the ice cream store)
large cardboard box and piece of cardboard
1 brass fastener
plastic lid
spool
glue
nail
tape
knife

What you do:

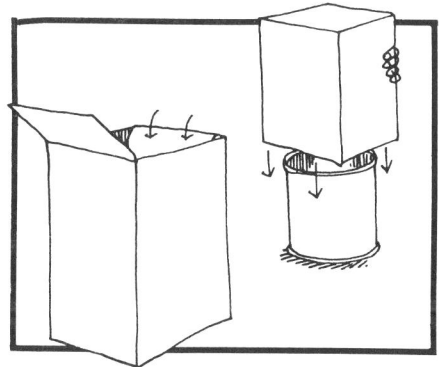

1 Tuck the flaps of the box inside it. Turn it upside down over the ice cream carton.

2 Cut a flap in the top of the box for the washing machine lid. Punch center hole in plastic lid with nail. This is the control knob.

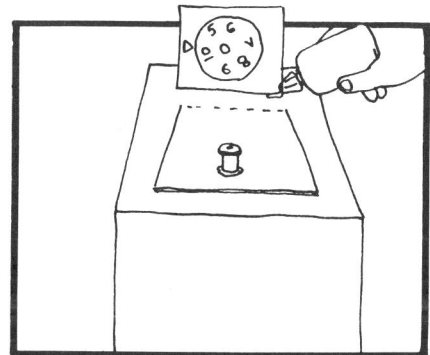

3 Glue the spool to this flap for a handle. Glue cardboard with control knob to box back so it sticks up. Put control knob on cardboard with brass fastener.

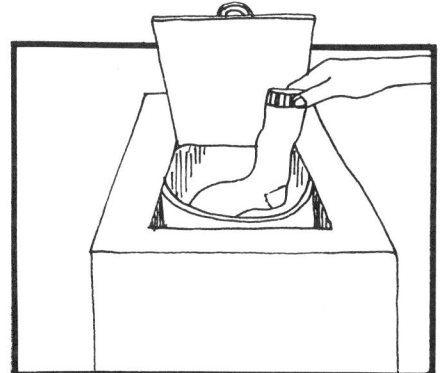

4 Open the machine and throw in the dirties.

What? We've lost a sock already?

85

Whirl-O

What you need:

string
button
scissors
crepe paper streamers, fat yarn or ribbons

What you do:

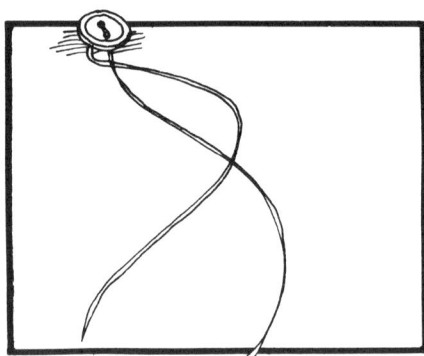

1 Tie some string onto the button, leaving two tails about as long as this page is from top to bottom.

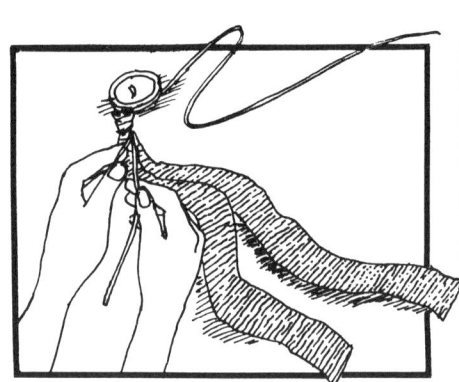

2 Knot the streamers onto one tail near the button.

3 Hold onto the other tail. Swing the streamers in any way, but don't swing near other people. And don't get dizzy!

If you go outdoors, you can run with your streamers but don't forget to watch where you go!

Wooden Spoon Doll

What you need:

permanent marker
wooden spoon
yarn
scissors
glue
handkerchief or cloth

What you do:

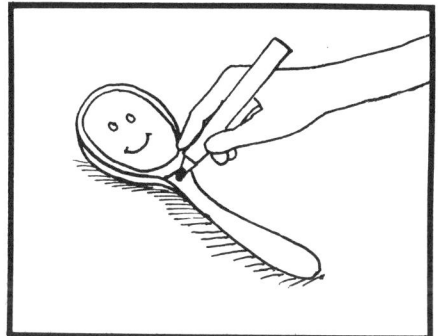

1 Draw a face on the round part of the spoon with a marker.

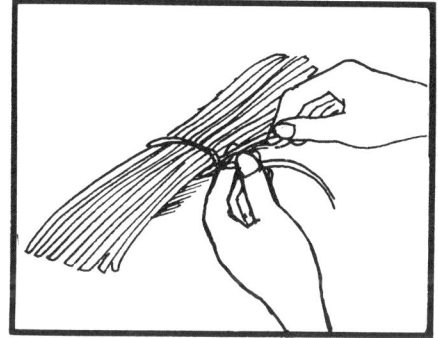

2 Cut pieces of yarn the same length. Tie the yarn in the middle to make the part in the doll's hair.

3 Glue the hair on the spoon, spreading it a bit to cover the wood.

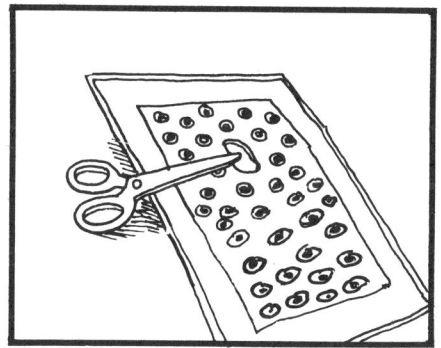

4 Cut a tiny hole in the middle of the handkerchief or circle of cloth.

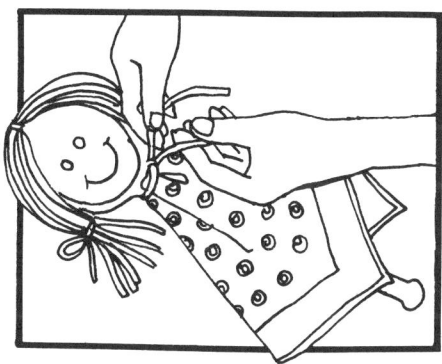

5 Slip the handkerchief onto the spoon handle and tie it in place with yarn.

Talk to your doll and tell each other secrets!

Writing Kit

What you need:

paper
scissors
watercolor pen
plain paper
pencil
small sponge
permanent marker
coffee can with see-through plastic lid
eraser

What you do:

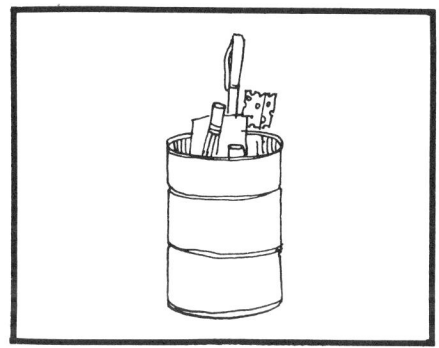

1 Into the coffee can put: pencil, eraser, plain paper, watercolor pen and a small sponge.

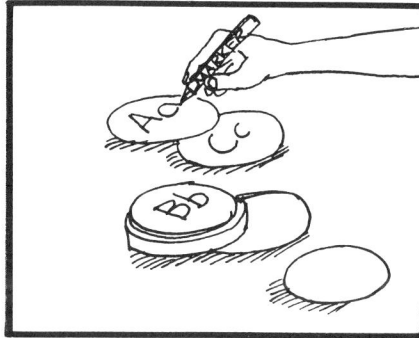

2 Make round circles from paper. Cut the circles to fit the coffee can lid.

3 Use the paper circles to make alphabet cards. Print a capital and a small letter on each card.

4 Put the coffee can lid over a letter card. Trace the letter onto the lid with the watercolor pen.

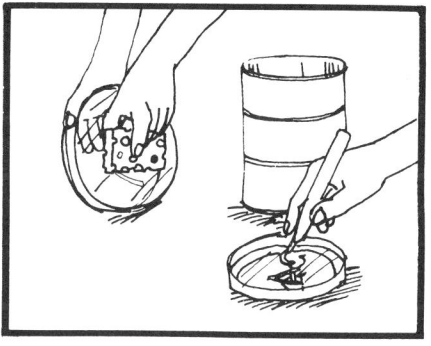

5 When you're finished, wipe the lid clean with a damp sponge. Do as many letters as you feel like.

Can you print your name?

SUPPLY CHEST

You can build up a collection of supplies for the things you can make using this book. In a big box you can save things like:

boxes
buttons
cardboard tubes
cereal boxes
coffee cans with lids
egg cartons
garbage bag ties (the jaggedy kind)
ice cream buckets with lids
L'eggs stockings eggs
magazines
margarine tubs with lids
peel-strip juice can lids
plastic bottles
plastic bowls with lids
plastic milk bottles with caps
plastic lids
popsicle sticks
scraps of cloth
shoelaces
sponges
spools (wooden if possible)
string
Styrofoam meat trays
yarn
and anything else that can be used safely

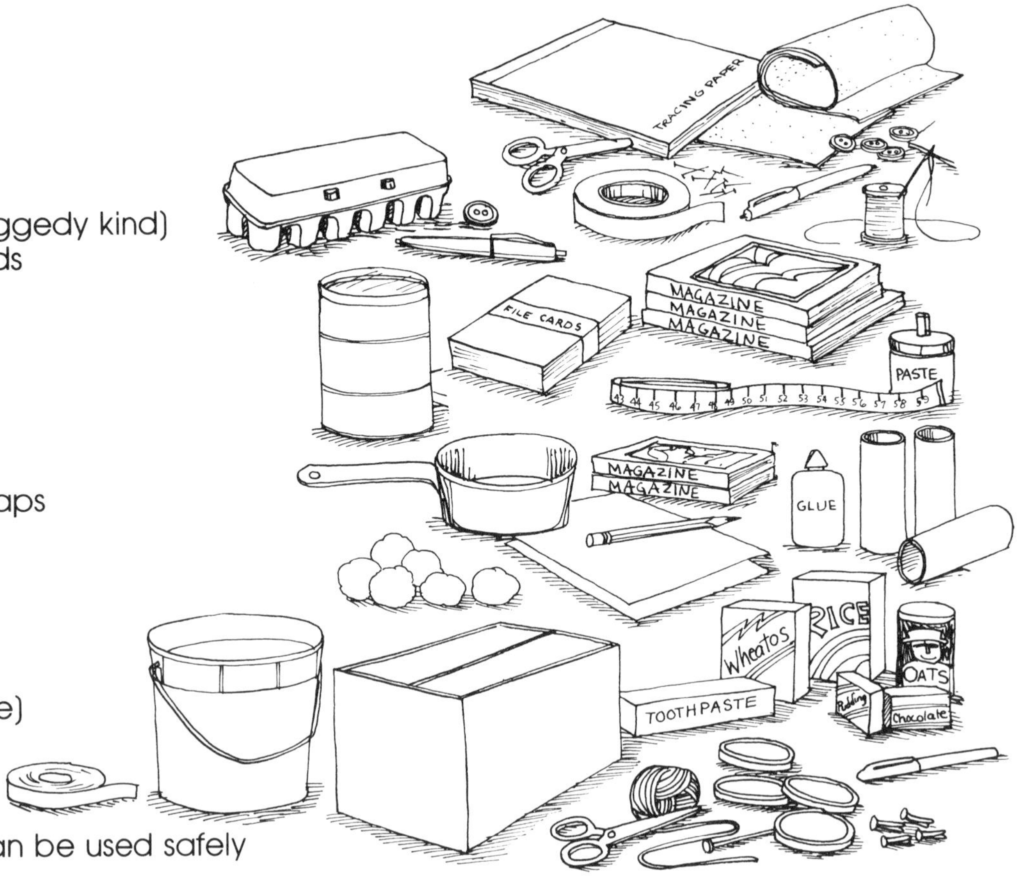

You may also want to make sure you have the following construction and game supplies in your chest:

brass fasteners
crayons
dice
file cards
knife
nails
paper (white and colored)
paste
pencils
pens (marking and ball-point)
scissors
tape

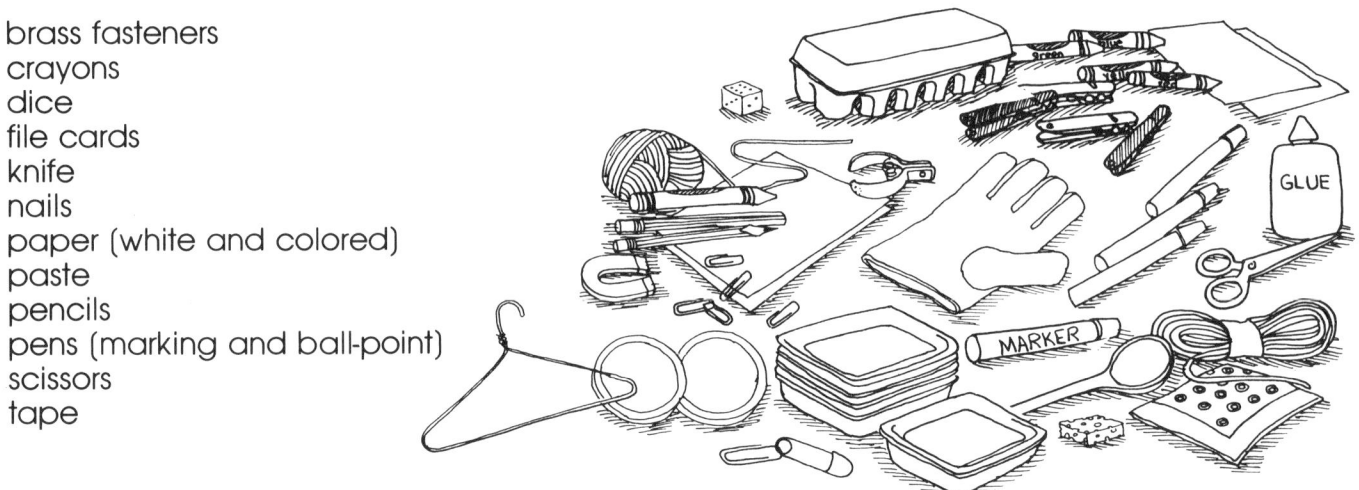

As your collection of supplies grows, you can get even more creative!